Fruit Fields in My Blood

Fruit Fields in My Blood

Okie Migrants in the West

Text by Toby F. Sonneman
Photographs by Rick Steigmeyer

University of Idaho Press
Moscow, Idaho

First published in 1992 by the University of Idaho Press, Moscow, Idaho 83843
© 1992 by Toby F. Sonneman and Rick Steigmeyer
"Pastures of Plenty," words and music by Woody Guthrie, © TRO 1960
(renewed 1988) and 1963 Ludlow Music, Inc., New York, NY, is here used
by permission.
Some names have been changed to protect the privacy of individuals.
Design by Karla Fromm
Printed in the United States of America
97 96 95 94 93 92   5 4 3 2 1

The Western States Book Awards are a project of the Western States Arts
Federation. The awards are supported by the Xerox Foundation, Crane
Duplicating Service, and the Witter Bynner Foundation for Poetry.
Additional Funding is provided by The National Endowment for the Arts
Literature Program.

Library of Congress Cataloging-in-Publication Data

Sonneman, Toby F., 1949–
    Fruit fields in my blood : Okie migrants in the West / text by Toby
F. Sonneman ; photographs by Rick Steigmeyer.
      p. cm.
    ISBN 0-89301-151-7. — ISBN 0-89301-152-5 (pbk.)
    1. Migrant agricultural laborers—West (U.S.) 2. Fruit trade—
West (U.S.)—Employees. I. Steigmeyer, Rick, 1947– .
II. Title
HD 1527.A17S66 1992
331.5′44′0978—dc20   91-3862
                       CIP

To Walter Williams and the other fruit pickers
whose sense of integrity and dignity in their work and lives
inspired us to write this book.

Pastures of Plenty

It's a mighty hard row that my poor hands have hoed;
My poor feet have traveled a hot dusty road,
Out of your dust bowl and westward we roll,
And your desert was hot and your mountain was cold.

I've worked in your orchards of peaches and prunes,
Slept on the ground in the light of the moon,
On the edge of your city you've seen us and then,
We come with the dust and we go with the wind.

California and Arizona, I make all your crops,
And it's up north to Oregon to gather your hops,
Dig the beets from your ground, cut the grapes from your vines,
To set on your tables your light sparkling wine.

Green pastures of plenty from dry, desert ground,
From that Grand Coulee Dam where the water runs down,
Every state in this Union us migrants have been,
We work in your fight, and we'll fight till we win.

Well, it's always we ramble, that river and I,
All along your green valley I'll work till I die,
My land I'll defend with my life, if it be,
'Cause my pastures of plenty must always be free.

———*©Woody Guthrie* (words and music)

Contents

Acknowledgments

This book owes its existence to the Okie fruit pickers who so generously shared their lives with us. Along with Walter Williams, we wish to thank especially Daniel and Darlene Williams and the whole extended Williams family, Bill and Vicki Taylor, James and Billie Griffin, Bill Wilson, Shorty, Marty Stone, Dale Jones, the Thomas family, the Browns, the O'Neils, the Spicers, the Englands, the O'Rears, and all the other fine people we met while on the fruit run.

We are very deeply indebted to Paul Wilderson and Marilyn Bacon Wilderson for their encouragement and steadfast faith in this book. Paul first saw the rough beginnings of the manuscript more than seven years ago as an editor at the University of Nebraska Press, and he helped enormously in the development of the text. Were it not for his continued interest, advice, and exhortations to be persistent in our search for a publisher, this project might have perished in a desk drawer.

Marilyn Bacon Wilderson has been an able and sensitive editor of the text and is a pleasure to work with. Her role in the final draft completed the circle of the book's long passage.

We also wish to express our gratitude to Jim Heaney, the director of the University of Idaho Press, for recognizing the potential of the book and for his helpfulness and encouragement in the rewriting of the manuscript.

A very special thanks goes to those who generously read and critiqued the manuscript: Molly See, Jack Johnson and Iris Gomez, and to Jane Cartwright, whose gift of a word processor and printer made our work infinitely easier. Last, but not least, we are very grateful to all our fine and loyal friends, who have been so constant in their support of this project.

Fruit Fields in My Blood
Introduction

1. Saving the Family Photographs
A Personal Introduction

A full sixteen years after my first apple harvest, I found myself on a ladder again, picking a particularly abundant crop of Golden apples. As I worked, I reflected on what had drawn me and my husband, Rick, to spend so many years of our lives as fruit pickers, and why it seemed so essential to give an account of our experiences.

Much had changed in those sixteen years since we began, but on that sunny day in October I was aware of how much had stayed the same. Physically I felt alternately exhilarated and exhausted by the hard work and the fresh air. Burdened with a heavy bag of apples that strained my back and shoulders as I walked to the bin, I often felt like a donkey carrying a load. But again on my ladder, looking out to the valley below

Left: *Picking buckets, Cashmere, Washington, 1972.*

filled with neat rows of fruit trees, and beyond to the snow-topped Cascade Mountains, I was awed by the beauty of this place. The apples themselves were lovely, a soft yellow color tinged with a rosy blush where the sunlight had left its mark. Although the physical work was hard and often monotonous, the surroundings made it a vastly more satisfying experience than factory work.

But it was later in the morning, when I'd stopped for a cup of coffee, that I was really reminded of why I'd been so drawn to this work. Rosie came by to chat with me. She had joined her husband, Bill, to work in supervising the harvest this year. Bill, originally from Oklahoma, had come to the Northwest as a child to pick fruit. Now he drove tractor and managed the orchard, but for decades he had made his living picking fruit, pruning, and thinning. He had a reputation as one of the fastest apple pickers around. Now his twenty-four-year-old son worked in the orchard and could pick as fast as Bill had.

Rosie started talking to me about an article Rick had written for the local newspaper, profiling several fruit pickers. One of them, she said, gave a bad image of pickers. In the article he'd complained about how little money he made and how hard it was to survive as a fruit picker. It made you feel depressed to read it, Rosie said, and that wasn't how she thought a picker ought to talk. "My family's always had a lot of pride in this work," Rosie asserted. "Billy's never been the sort to whine about anything, and if the day ever comes where he really feels bad about bein' in the orchard, well, that'll be the day he quits doin' this kind of work."

Rosie's argument moved me, bringing back all my years of living among fruit pickers and getting to know their ways. It reminded me why after reading John Steinbeck's *Grapes of*

Right: *Al Gage, Monitor, Washington, September 1974.*

Wrath in my youth I was so attracted to the migratory life and so glad to find that the people Steinbeck wrote about still existed. For all its hardships—low pay, low status, back-breaking work, and often poor conditions in the field and inadequate housing—most of the people who work in the fields and the orchards are not downtrodden, beaten individuals. "Fruit tramps" they call themselves mockingly, aware that mainstream society has derogatorily labeled them "tramps." Although they are regarded with disdain and encouraged by schools, communities, and government organizations to leave agricultural work rather than to improve it, these people have miraculously clung to their self-respect, believing in the dignity and value of their work. A sense of pride sustains them.

I am more realistic now than I was sixteen years ago when I had a somewhat romantic notion of migratory life, but the migrants' strong sense of pride still impresses me. It's what struck me when I first read *The Grapes of Wrath* in high school and wished I could know people like that—people who had such integrity and compassion for others that they could rise above the harsh way they were treated. Recently, rereading Steinbeck with the added perspective of years spent living and working with Okie migrants, I hear the ring of truth and accuracy in the voices and descriptions of the Joads. These were people who refused to be ashamed of the poverty and hardships that they endured; they would not think like victims, and they deplored any media reports that depicted them as "sorry, low-down fruit tramps."

The Okies were not my people, and though reading *The Grapes of Wrath* had awakened a longing to know the people Steinbeck wrote of, I thought that people like that had disappeared with the Great Depression. Becoming a fruit picker was

not even a remote possibility for a Jewish high school student living on Chicago's South Side. It was not until I got to college that I could legitimize my interest in people with an academic term: anthropology. Like many of my generation, I was in college to learn for learning's sake, rather than to find a career. I knew I wanted to travel and I was very interested in migratory people. Independently, I read everything I could about Gypsies, and I got to know and photograph some Gypsies in the United States and Europe. But they had a distrust of a young *gaji* (Romani for a female "non-Gypsy") that kept me at a distance, and I realized that I couldn't get to know these people more deeply at that time in my life.

For several years I alternated adventure and travel with short stints at jobs to get by financially. In 1972 I was in limbo, without work or enough money to travel again. I was living in a dreary warehouselike structure in San Francisco with an assorted group of friends and strangers. Every day I'd go out to stand in long lines and fill out forms for the lowest paid jobs. Despite my college education, my lack of experience in clerking, filing, or typing made the possibility of employment remote. It seemed time to leave the city, and when somebody mentioned that there were apricots to pick up north, I began to dream again of being a fruit picker.

Leaving my belongings at the San Francisco warehouse, I packed a small backpack and hitchhiked north. Rick joined me in Oregon, quitting his hated job at a pulp mill. He packed some clothes, a camera, and a blanket into his old VW bug and together we continued north. In Seattle we made inquiries at the employment office. We were told there were picking jobs around Wenatchee, about 120 miles east of Seattle, so we traveled over the mountains, across Stevens Pass. It was one of the most beautiful trips I have ever taken. Waterfalls rushed down the Cascade Mountains, which separated the rainy western side of

Washington from the drier hills and orchard country of central Washington.

In Peshastin, a tiny logging and orchard town nestled in the foothills of the Cascades, we found our first job. The lean old farmer in striped overalls who hired us led us to the cabin where we could stay while we worked. It was a simple two-room cabin. The kitchen was equipped with a woodstove and a hotplate, an old wooden table, and some battered pots and pans. The bedroom had a big, creaky double bed and a cot. In back of the cabin was a bathroom with a shower and toilet. That was a rare feature in a picker's cabin and seemed luxurious; later we were to live in several picker's cabins with no facilities other than an outside water faucet and an outhouse.

Our first work was thinning. In early summer when the tiny apples and pears hang from the trees in clusters, it is time to thin them out, breaking up the clusters and spacing the fruit apart. The worker drops the smaller fruit to the ground so the remaining fruit can grow larger.

The work itself was simple, but learning to manage the ladders we used to reach the tops of the trees was often a challenge. The three-legged ladders were a nightmare to move on the steep foothill orchards.

We worked through the thinning season, then waited out the hot weeks of July and August while the fruit grew larger. We walked around the dry hills, swam in the icy river and the irrigation canals, and tasted tiny fresh strawberries from the farmer's garden and thick cream we bought from a neighbor. In mid-August we found another job and cabin and began the pear harvest, going to work at dawn, subjecting our backs to the strain of carrying the heavy bags of fruit.

By the time we were picking apples, the scorching summer days had cooled into crisp autumn ones. On frosty mornings we started to work at eight or nine, boosted by hot cups of coffee

View from an apple picker's cabin, Cashmere, Washington, 1972.

Right: *Filling the bin with Red Delicious apples, Okanogan County, Washington, 1978.*

and cocoa. The work was never easy, but it began to have a rhythm and a pace that was becoming natural to us. The periods of total leisure in between the jobs, the breaks for coffee or lunch that had the qualities of a picnic in the orchard, and the seasonal changes in the work and the weather made us feel integrated with the land and the seasons and seduced us into the fruit-

picker way of life. Soon we were thinking of the next season, the next job, the next fruit to pick.

We began to meet people who were unlike the more settled people in a community. The migrants were free of the stresses and constraints of highly structured time, the appropriate dress required for higher-status jobs, or the acquisition and upkeep of all the trappings of middle-class life. Most of the pickers we met were *Okies*—a mixture of people whose parents had left Oklahoma, Arkansas, Texas, and Missouri to follow the crops in the 1930s. They had a distinct way of speaking that was often humorous and unexpectedly eloquent and a connection with their extended families that was unusual in the West. Their hardiness and sense of humor seemed to pull them through the worst circumstances intact and always made a good story later. We found the Okies to be great storytellers, and the tales they told of their varied experiences lured us into trying the fruit run.

Citrus picker, Winterhaven, Florida, January 1974.

After that first season in Washington, we traveled south to Florida to pick oranges and grapefruit. Here we experienced some of the worst elements of the migrant's world. The work was incredibly hard. It took me most of that first season in Florida to learn to move the heavy wooden twenty-foot ladders just a few inches at a time so they wouldn't topple over. As I am just over five feet tall, the ladders towered over me. The weighty citrus fruit grew on tall trees with thorns so treacherous that pickers had to wear thick leather gloves to protect their hands. Picked fruit was carried in huge bags with one strap across the neck and shoulder, a bag design that eventually crippled the older workers. The sandy orchards, called *groves* in the South, were a nightmare of biting insects, ants, and spiders. Cars got stuck in the loose sand, and it was a challenge to walk in the sand carrying ladders and heavy bags of fruit.

On top of this, the crews were incredibly inefficient: sometimes we spent days waiting for a bin in which to dump our fruit, while the crew boss and the tractor driver played endless games of cards. The crew bosses in Florida were often dishonest and exploitive, especially on the "wino" crew we worked with our first year there.

Perhaps worst of all was the prejudice and hostility of the surrounding community. We were denied motel rooms, use of public restrooms, and apartment rental when it was known that we picked fruit, and we soon learned to hide our occupation. The rampant discrimination gave us a small taste of what life is like for the black people in the South, for whom fruit picking is one of the only forms of employment. Crews were basically segregated, with the exception of one fully integrated crew that held a union contract: the United Farm Workers crew for Coca Cola (Minute Maid). Although as whites we were able to find work with crews that were otherwise all black, we saw few other whites interested in doing this, and we suspected that a

black person would not have the same freedom to work on a white crew.

But even in Florida, where conditions were the worst, both black and white fruit pickers reflected a pride in their work. As Rick worked alongside other pickers, he often asked if he could take their pictures. These early photos were often self-consciously posed as the pickers tried to look their best for the portraits. Yet the poses they struck accurately revealed their self-perceptions. With straightened backs, their shoulders arched back and their heads held high, the pickers would look piercingly into the lens of the camera. They were often on or next to their ladder. Never once was there any expression of shame or disgrace in the work that they were doing. And as recently as last fall, when I went around the orchard taking pictures of the apple pickers, many of whom were Hispanic, the pose was the same, as if their sense of pride crossed all cultural lines.

Our first winter in Florida, after much persistence, we were lucky enough to get a job on the UFW crew (we tried to get on the next winter as well, but as migrants we had lost our seniority). There we met Walter Jay Williams, a thirty-five-year-old steward for the union. Walter was an Okie from a small community in Texas. When he was a boy his father had built a camper from flattened tin cans, and with the camper nailed to a wooden frame on the back of a Model T Ford pickup truck, he had taken the family to California to pick cotton, peas, and fruit. Walter's mother had a collection of old photographs from that time, and years later Walter borrowed the photos from his mother so that Rick could make copies of them for the rest of the family. These photographs were a treasured record of the family's journey west and the roots of their new lives as migrant fruit pickers in the 1940s and 1950s.

Left: *Walter Williams, Omak, Washington, 1978.*

The Williams children and a Spartan trailer in the early 1950s.
From the album of Osie and Josephine Williams.

Walter liked to tell a story about the time when he was a boy and the trailer they were then living in veered off the road as they drove around a difficult curve on a mountain pass. Their possessions were scattered about the road and the family surveyed the wreckage with dismay. But Walter's mother, wasting no time, ran down the road to rescue the family photographs that had tumbled out of their box before the relentless wind blew them away forever. The image of this story stayed with us, a symbolic message of the importance of remembering the history and experiences of these people.

Walter himself was an endless source of stories and experiences, a wealth of oral history. He had been a preacher in Texas and he had a strong sense of righteousness and religious values. He was unusually well read and open minded and his vision of fruit picking as dignified work made him an eloquent speaker for other migrants. In Florida he seemed in his element as a union organizer, using the style and the language of preaching to motivate both the blacks and the whites on the crew who protested union dues even though their wages were double those of nonunion crews.

After meeting Walter, we often went to visit him and his family, and they welcomed us with a generous hospitality. Walter, Mattie, and their six tow-haired children lived in a mobile home on the outskirts of a little town. Walter told us that he wasn't able to make the payments on the mobile home—he'd probably let it just "go back." Anyway, he wanted to travel again. He spoke longingly of cherry picking and told us of the places in California, Oregon, and Washington where they'd picked. "Once those cherries start bloomin', you couldn't hardly keep me here," Walter said.

We left Florida in the early spring with no more money than we'd come with. We felt lucky to have enough to leave on. We weren't too serious about fruit picking yet, so we took odd jobs in California and visited friends there.

June came, and we weren't committed to other jobs or settled in a particular place. We remembered what Walter had said about cherry picking and we wondered if we could really make money picking them. We traveled to Kennewick, in southern Washington, and began looking for jobs. We remembered Walter talking about a good cherry-picking job he had for a Japanese orchardist in Kennewick, but we had no idea how to find him. The orchards were widely scattered around a large area, and we hardly knew how to look for a job. We were outside town, filling our car with gas and wondering where to go next, when a pickup truck and a camper pulled up near us. The children's heads poking out the window reminded us uncannily

Right: *Migrant-built trailer, Kennewick, Washington, 1974.*

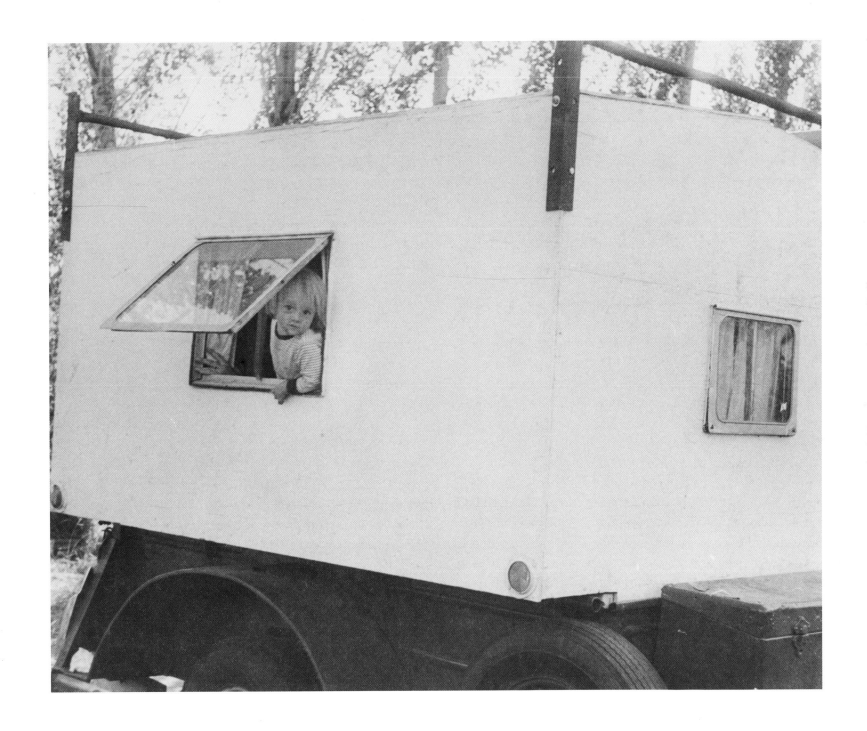

of Walter's kids. Taking a long shot, we asked the driver of the truck if he knew of them. Yes, he answered, he was Walter's cousin, and he gave us directions to the orchard where Walter was working. Although this seemed to us a fortuitous chance meeting, we later realized that Walter and his cousin James (whom we later came to know as well) saw nothing remarkable in the event. There were so many interrelations between families on the migrant run that they assumed you could eventually find anyone you were looking for. For us, however, since we had no knowledge or experience in the orchards and no connections to other fruit pickers, the coincidence seemed providential.

Walter was delighted to see us, and he managed to get us a job at the orchard he was working in. We parked our VW van alongside the trailers and buses and tents and set up our camp. In the morning Billy, the foreman, showed us where to pick and found ladders and buckets for us. After struggling for half a day only filling a few boxes, while we watched pickers around us fill stacks of boxes with cherries, we found Walter and his family and asked for help. We spent some time just watching them while they gave us tips on cherry picking. By the next day, our boxes were stacking up faster, although it looked as if we'd never catch up to the pickers who'd been at it for years.

After working in Kennewick, we found out about other cherry jobs in the Northwest and tried to work with the Williams family whenever we could. Our affinity with this extended family developed as we continued to spend time around them. Sharing coffee breaks and lunch breaks in the orchard, spending afternoons after work, playing and reading with the children, and listening to Walter's stories in the evening, we grew very close to them.

As we were becoming drawn into the cycles of the fruit run, the Williamses were unofficially adopting us into their family. We met Walter's younger brother Daniel; his wife, Darlene;

and their six children. Daniel's family also picked fruit and often parked their trailer right next to Walter's in the migrant camp. Despite the differences in their styles, the two families lived close to each other, without much privacy, in relative harmony. Later we met another of Walter's brothers, Paul. He lived in Texas and had to be on a kidney-dialysis machine, but he loved to pick fruit and missed it so much that one year he came out to pick for a week with his wife, Bonnie, and their two children. He thought cherry picking was worth the long trip from Texas to Washington, even though he had to spend two of the days in Washington traveling more than a hundred miles from the cherry orchard to be hooked up to the nearest dialysis machine. Paul's obvious attachment to fruit picking was a stunning example of the pickers' attitudes toward their work. It differed greatly from what we'd been led to expect. These were not people forced into agricultural work by unfortunate circumstances. These were people making a choice, valuing the opportunity to stay connected with their families. They were choosing a way of life considered to be without merit by the rest of society.

In the years that followed, we became initiated into the migrant culture through Walter, his family, and friends. We saved our picking money to buy our own first trailer—a little sixteen-footer from the 1950s—which we pulled with a 1956 pink and white Buick. The wooden interior of the trailer made us feel like we were living in the hollow of a tree. With a little dining booth, a compact kitchen, and a bed—all within arm's reach—the trailer was cozy and functional, and we discovered how much we liked the freedom of our own migratory home.

We wintered in Florida, Texas, Arizona, and Washington. Every year we hitched up our trailer in late April or early May and traveled to California for the first of the cherries, then followed the fruit as it ripened up north and east to Montana. We picked prunes, pears, and apples in central Washington and

Cherry orchard, Wenatchee Heights, Washington, 1973.

illegal aliens, most of them workers from Mexico, and they became the preferred choice for cheap, reliable labor.

In 1975, we helped form Migrant Workers of America, an advocate group for migrants. We hoped that fair legislation could preserve the jobs and lifestyle so crucial to this culture. We continued the organization for several years, learning some difficult lessons in the process. Few legislators cared about migrants; because they were migratory they were not represented by any particular political candidate, and often they did not vote at all. Migrants had difficulty planning where they would be at election time in order to establish state residency in advance. This, coupled with their alienation from local issues and politics, proved to be a real obstacle in our discussions with legislators. In any case, fair legislation began to seem impossible; as workers of different races were pitted against each other, the real issues were obscured. And finally, Okie migrants were among the least organizable of groups—they were too suspicious of organization and too protective of their individual independence to participate in group action. These conflicting factors began to undermine the intent of the organization, and in 1978 the group disbanded.

We continued to pick fruit, however, and in the spring of 1979 our first child was born. We took him with us to the cherry orchard in Kennewick when he was just six weeks old. Our new definition as a fruit-picking family deepened our acceptance and involvement with other fruit pickers. At last our co-workers realized that we weren't picking fruit as a lark or a fill-in job, or as a means to writing a book. Despite our cultural, educational, and hereditary differences we had become, like them, wed to the seasons and the life of the fruit run.

In recent years we have watched and have been affected by the dying of that lifestyle. Orchards have been gobbled up by subdivisions and condominiums with names like "Cherry Tree Acres." Small growers with personal relationships to the work-

stayed until the cold and the lack of work drove us south again.

Most of our jobs were only a couple of weeks long, but we came back to the places that had been good to us year after year. We worked with many people that we knew and met new ones at each job. We were amazed at the interconnected relations of the people who worked the fruit. It seemed like a large extended family. We were continually reminded how many people picked fruit because they loved it—not because they had to.

Times were changing for the fruit pickers though. Jobs were getting scarce, real wages lowering. The growers in northern California and the Northwest had increased their use of

ers are forced to sell out, and agribusiness conglomerates take over. Workers are no longer valued for their reliability in coming back year after year or for picking the fruit with care. With lowered wages, and large numbers of recent immigrants who desperately need work, many Okie migrants have been pushed out of fruit work. Often they are unable to find jobs in orchards where they have previously worked. Contractors supply a large grower with a ready crew, and often such contractors favor non-English–speaking workers because they are frequently in a position where they must accept less than adequate conditions and wages.

The situation in farm work changes year by year as new immigration laws are enacted, affecting the use of illegal workers, but many of the people we worked with in the fruit orchards have left, finally discouraged by lack of work and the drop in wages. Many of them have returned to Texas, Oklahoma, Arkansas, and Missouri, where land is still cheap and they are among their own people. Daniel Williams returned to Texas with his wife, Darlene, to pursue his occupation as a roofer. Walter Williams also left the fruit run many years ago. After his marriage to Mattie broke apart, he became a traveling preacher once again in Texas and later happily remarried. Now, as an ordained minister with a church in Artesia, New Mexico, he feels he has found his true calling. A recent letter from him demonstrates that he still retains a strong feeling for his fruit-picker past. "Even if the years have separated me from the fruit fields of my childhood, they can never take them out of my blood," he wrote, "because it flows in my veins like life itself."

Other fruit pickers have settled in the West, in towns in California, Oregon, Washington, and Idaho, finding other kinds of work to sustain them and perhaps still picking fruit in the summer. Even those who leave are often drawn back temporarily, their fingers itching to pick fruit again, their spirits eager for the expansive freedom of the road. We are now among this group of fruit pickers. Rick is a journalist for a small-town newspaper in Washington, and I am an independent writer and artisan. But every summer I drive to the surrounding cherry orchards at the break of dawn—4:30 A.M.—and slip into my old harness and bucket for the yearly ritual of cherry picking. There are always familiar faces in the orchard, people we have known for fifteen years or more. We've watched their children grow, and they have known our children since they were babies lying under the fruit trees.

Perhaps they are ordinary people, but in the context of our changing society they seem extraordinary—remarkable for their wit, perceptiveness, and ability to survive. In keeping this account of their stories, comments, and photographs, we've often been reminded of Walter's mother, running down the road to save the family photographs before they blew away. Much of this way of life has been eroded, leaving only the memories. We have tried to make those memories and past experiences as tangible as the family photo album. As Walter writes, "Just knowing that there was such a life and I was a part of it is reason enough to feel a sense of pride."

Left: *Even if the years have separated me from the fruit fields of my childhood, they can never take them out of my blood."*
Crescent Bar, Washington, 1982.

2. "It Just Gets in Your Blood"
History of Okie Migrants

In the summer of 1937, an old Model A Ford sputtered down U.S. Route 66, from Oklahoma to California. A family of twelve was squeezed inside—parents with gaunt, weathered faces and rough hands, ten blond and scrawny children. The outside of the jalopy was heaped with chairs and mattresses, pots and pans. Conspicuously poor and newly migrant, this family was one of the tens of thousands of "Dust Bowl refugee" families who streamed into California's fields and orchards looking for work. Like the Joads in *The Grapes of Wrath*, they were to be subjected to more poverty and hardships as they adapted to a new way of life picking the crops of a bountiful western agriculture.

Some forty years later, one of these ten children, now a grown man, pulls his pickup truck with a camper and trailer into

Left: *Pea picking, the late 1940s.*
From the album of Osie and Josephine Williams.

the Mount Shasta rest area on U.S. 5, between California and Oregon. Thirty feet of white and green corrugated aluminum gleam from the new Terry trailer, indistinguishable from any of the tourist-owned trailers in the rest area. The family emerging from the pickup and camper is larger than most, and their faces suggest that they have known harder times. But their dress is distinctively middle America, from the racks of K-Mart and J. C. Penney. When they talk, there is a southern twang and a quaintness of speech that betrays its origin in the language of the Okie migrants of the 1930s and 1940s. But these people are modern-day "fruit tramps" who follow the harvest through the western states, descendants of the hardy Dust Bowl migrants.

Since the Great Depression little has been heard of the Okie migrants. They are considered extinct, as if all the poor white southern migrants had been absorbed into America's melting pot. Like the family with the new pickup and trailer, they seem invisible, but they blend in with the larger culture in appearance only. Their work, lifestyles, backgrounds, and values reveal stark contrasts with middle America. Cultural assumptions of an educated, middle-class society have often prevented Okie migrants from being understood or visible beyond the images from the Great Depression. Yet many Okies have remained in agricultural work by choice rather than by economic bondage, carving a unique niche in the history of agricultural labor.

Even before the Dust Bowl migration of the 1930s, there were Anglos from the Great Plains who followed the harvests. Migratory agricultural labor in the United States originated with the wheat harvest in the mid-1800s. In "Origins of Migratory Labor," Paul Taylor describes that period:

Right: *Apple picker, Peshastin, Washington, 1973.*

In deciding what to plant in the Spring, men began to turn away from mixed farming—the traditional balance of crops adjusted to family labor. They began to specialize in wheat. [As a result, a farmer's] ability to harvest . . . was coming to depend less on the sweat of his brow and the help of family and neighbors and more on the availability and goodwill of itinerant temporary workers. . . . The laborers they sought were no longer 'hired men' engaged for the year to work steadily, each one beside a working farmer; now they were extra hands wanted at harvest time only.[1]

Specialization in wheat reached California about 1860 and lasted about twenty years. Wheat growers in California had an advantage over those in the Great Plains: they had a ready supply of Chinese laborers. When California growers switched to fruit and vegetable crops, there was plenty of available labor for the harvests.

The wheat harvest in the Midwest continued to demand seasonal laborers. Walter Williams, whose Texan father was one of those migrants, recalls, "A lot of the fruitpickers started out following the wheat harvest. And back in those days, the early twenties, there weren't very many farms around. So most of those people would ride the freight trains all over the United States, wherever the wheat was."

Meanwhile, in California the agricultural potential of the land was being exploited to a new level. Transcontinental railroads and refrigeration cars opened up new markets. Irrigation made more land available for crops. As specialized crops grew larger and larger, the demand for seasonal labor increased accordingly. The bulk of the labor was performed by the Chinese until 1882, when Congress ended Chinese immigration by the passage of the Chinese Exclusion Act. Japanese, Hindu, Filipino and Mexican laborers were employed on California farms

Harvesting wheat, circa the 1920s.
From the album of Osie and Josephine Williams.

around the turn of the century. It was easy for Mexicans to cross the border for work, and by 1917, Mexican workers were legally admitted for temporary employment in agriculture, mines, and railroads. In the 1920s, California tripled its Mexican population, and the United States absorbed a million Mexican people.

As farms and orchards increased in size and more and more seasonal laborers were employed from groups of Asian and Mexican immigrants, the potential for the exploitation of agricultural workers grew. "Now farming became an industry, and the owners followed Rome, although they did not know it. They imported slaves, although they did not call them slaves: Chinese, Japanese, Mexicans, Filipinos. They live on rice and beans, the business men said. They don't need much. They wouldn't know what to do with good wages. Why, look how they live. Why, look what they eat. And if they get funny—deport them," Steinbeck wrote in *The Grapes of Wrath*.[2]

The Immigration Law of 1924 stopped most of the immigration from Europe and Asia, and Mexicans became the dominant farm laborers. They were preferred over other workers for their willingness to work cheaply and for the ease of deporting them. In the winter months, when farm laborers were no longer needed, immigration authorities deported them en masse to Mexico at taxpayers' expense. A lemon grower in Whittier wrote, "Mexicans as a rule work quietly and uncomplainingly and are well satisfied with wages and conditions. When a troublemaker appears, he is discharged at once." In contrast, he described the behavior of Anglo workers as "crabbing, grumbling, ill-natured complaining of conditions."[3]

The Williams family and their trailer, the 1950s.
From the album of Osie and Josephine Williams.

The depression of the thirties brought a deluge of Anglo workers and provoked a trend of reverse migration back to Mexico. From the whole United States half a million Mexicans returned to their country of origin.

A combination of poor conditions among farmers and farm workers in the Great Plains forced Anglo migrants to the West Coast in the 1930s. Mechanization reduced the need for agricultural workers; the crop curtailment policies of the New Deal paid subsidies to owners but not to tenants or agricultural laborers. Landowners soon realized that they could use the government payments received for reductions in crop production to buy tractors that would replace their tenants. Thus tenants who may have farmed the land for generations were forced off the land, "tractored out."

"Families who had lived for many years on the little 'croppers lands' were dispossessed because the land was in the

Brother Johnson's Bible class, the 1950s.
From the album of Osie and Josephine Williams.

hands of banks and the finance companies and because these owners found that one man with a tractor could do the work of ten sharecropper families. Faced with the question of starving or moving, these dispossessed families came west," wrote Steinbeck in *Their Blood Is Strong*, an informative pamphlet published in 1938.[4] Drought, dust storms, a depressed economy, and unemployment all contributed to drive these people to seek new opportunities in the West.

"My father was a foreman on the oil rigs in Oklahoma," Bill recalled. "During the Depression, they closed the whole operation down. After he lost his job, he came out to California in 1934. He drove a '31 Chevy out west, with three little kids."

"And then the dispossessed were drawn west," Steinbeck wrote in *The Grapes of Wrath*:

From Kansas, Oklahoma, Texas, New Mexico; from Nevada and Arkansas families, tribes, dusted out, tractored out. Carloads, caravans, homeless and hungry; twenty thousand and fifty thousand and a hundred thousand and two hundred thousand. They streamed over the mountains, hungry and restless—restless as ants, scurrying to find work to do—to lift, to push, to pull, to pick, to cut—anything, any burden to bear, for food. The kids are hungry. We got no place to live. Like ants scurrying for work, for food, and most of all, for land. . . . Okies—the owners hated them because the owners knew they were soft and the Okies strong, that they were fed and the Okies hungry.[5]

The term *Okie* became attached to Anglo migrants of the Depression era and acquired the stigma that Californians associated with migrant pickers. In *The Grapes of Wrath* a migrant who's already worked in California explains the term to Tom Joad, newly arrived. "Well, Okie use' ta mean you was from Oklahoma. Now it means you're a dirty son of a bitch. Okie means you're scum. Don't mean nothing itself, it's the way they

Sorting peas, the late 1940s.
From the album of Osie and Josephine Williams.

say it."[6] Gerald Haslam describes the evolution of the term in an article entitled "What about the Okies?"

While Oklahoma and Oklahomans were the focus of attention, the actual migrants drifted in from across the Great Plains, north and south: the Dakotas, Nebraska, Kansas, Missouri, Oklahoma, Texas and Arkansas mainly. . . . The word "Okie" has been traced back to 1905, but its use as a generally derogatory term for any white migrant in the 1930's stuck. . . . Fittingly, it has been the recent work of second-generation Okies—especially Merle Haggard and Buck Owens—that has re-introduced pride in the term, though many contemporary Oklahomans remain resentful over its use to describe "depression drifters."[7]

The Williams family in the fields, California, the 1950s.
From the album of Osie and Josephine Williams.

The term "Okies" is useful to describe Anglo migrants, and it has generally lost its derogatory connotation.

The Okies who came west in the thirties were largely destitute, making them vulnerable to exploitation. The unscrupulous practices in agriculture included overhiring to reduce payment and shorten employment, dishonest scales and means of payment, and charges for rent and food bought at overpriced "company stores." Besides being exploited on the job, because of their desire for land and work, the Okies were easy targets for unscrupulous business operations that John Blanchard calls "gypo enterprises" run by smooth-talking operators: "To them, the home-seeking, job-hunting migrant is a sucker to be exploited." Advertisements for cheap land lured Okies into buying "stump ranches," which were expensive to clear and had poor soil, or farms that needed expensive irrigation to be produc-

tive. Growers in California and in the Northwest advertised abundant jobs for pickers; by the time migrants arrived all the jobs had long been filled, and often the harvest was over.[8]

"The exploitation of migrants is but a phase of a more serious situation," asserted John Blanchard in *Caravans to the Northwest*, published in 1940. Migrants who cannot find work also find the usual kinds of unemployment assistance closed to them. Because of their status as nonresidents, they are denied community health and medical services, are not eligible for old-age assistance benefits, and cannot vote. Unions worried about an oversupply of workers causing lower wages may deny migrants membership.[9]

In one important way, the Okies were different from the groups of migrants that preceded them. As American citizens, they could not be deported, although the state patrol made attempts to bar them from the state of California. They also had a tendency to settle down in California's communities, to the dismay of local townspeople. The Okie migrants congregated in segregated ghettos that were called "Little Oklahomas," or "Hoovervilles."

A picker we knew recalled the migrant camps he had experienced: "There used to be what was known as tent cities. There may be forty acres of ground just covered with tents, where people come in to pick a harvest, like peas for instance. And there'd just be acres of these white tents. Living conditions were just terrible, but you have to remember that was back in the Great Depression, and very few people had a really good living then. People didn't really object to it that much because they weren't that far below the rest of the people."

Growers in the Northwest too were unprepared for the flood of migratory workers and rarely provided adequate housing. "Rural slums sprout like mushrooms during the harvesting season," reported John Blanchard in 1940. "Families unable to afford tents use old junk, burlap, and paper cartons in the building of their temporary homes. To squatters' homes like these, come increasing numbers of drought refugees. . . . Here, sickness is a frequent uninvited guest."[10]

Franklin D. Roosevelt responded to the problems of dispossessed tenant farmers by creating the Resettlement Administration in 1935, an agency that used various programs in an attempt to resettle displaced farmers. Most of these programs were later transferred to a new agency, the Farm Security Administration. As a response to growing concern about the poor living conditions of migratory workers, the Farm Security Administration initiated the construction and operation of a series of model farm-labor camps in the mid 1930s.

"They provide wooden shelters and tent platforms, sanitary toilets and shower baths," detailed John Blanchard in 1940, after the first of these camps had been established in the Pacific

Migrant camp, California, the late 1940s.
From the album of Osie and Josephine Williams.

Northwest. FSA camps were also established in California, Texas, Arizona, Florida, and New York. Blanchard goes on to list the improved facilities for migrant workers: "an assembly hall, small clinic with a registered nurse in attendance, an isolation ward, . . . a central utility building, water distribution system, . . . sewage disposal plants, . . . facilities for washing clothes by hand, . . . adequate space for the all-essential migrant's car . . . a nursery and kindergarten . . . for pre-school children."[11]

In *The Grapes of Wrath* a migrant child speaks with awe of an FSA camp: "Oh, you never seen anything so nice. Got a place for the kids to play, an' them toilets with paper. Pull down a little jigger an' the water comes right in the toilet; an' they ain't no cops let to come look in your tent any time they want, an' the fella runs the camp is so polite, comes a-visitin' an' talks an' ain't high an' mighty. . . . Why, God Awmighty, they got hot water right in pipes, an' you get in under a shower bath an' it's warm. You never seen such a place."[12] Admission to the camp was open only to experienced farm workers with families. Single men were not accepted. Families were required to have a physical examination to enter a camp. The cost per day for a family was ten cents, and residents were expected to help keep the camp clean.[13]

The model camps could serve only a fraction of the migrant population, but they demonstrated what could be done to drastically improve a crisis situation. Most radical was the management of the camps: "In each camp, the worker is permitted a voice in the way it should be governed. . . . Camps are divided into districts with one representative elected by the workers from each district." This representative governing council discussed and voted on issues such as labor meetings in the camp, expenditures from the camp fund or the distribution of handbills within the camp.[14] "The result of this self-government has been remarkable," wrote Steinbeck in *Their Blood Is Strong*. "The inhabitants of the camp came there beaten, sullen, and destitute. But as their social sense was revived they have settled down."[15]

The FSA camps were really a socialist, utopian experiment, and as such they provoked fears that the democratic methods of camp management would open the door to labor union organization. "Many people eye them as the gathering places for a worthless lot of drifters and agitators bent upon stirring up labor unrest and strikes," wrote John Blanchard.[16] Though the program survived such opposition, it did not withstand the postwar economy drive of the 1940s. In the late forties,

Pea pickers, California, the late 1940s.
From the album of Osie and Josephine Williams.

all the camps were liquidated or sold. Such farsighted programs as schools, recreational facilities, clinics, and housing and sanitation standards were also ended. Today there are migrant camps little improved over those squatters' camps described in 1940; now they are usually inhabited by Hispanic workers.

The Resettlement Administration, and later the Farm Security Administration, needed public support of its programs to help tenant farmers. Because there was little public awareness of the problem, the "Historical Section" of the FSA was established, to photograph and document the plight of the tenant farmer. Under the extraordinary leadership of Roy Stryker, such great documentary photographers as Dorthea Lange, Walker Evans, Arthur Rothstein, Ben Shahn, Russell Lee, and others produced a remarkable collection of 270,000 pictures. Many of these were published in newspapers across the nation and magazines such as *Life*, *Look*, and *Survey Graphic*. The photographs stunned the nation with their stark look at the poverty and harsh conditions of the dispossessed. They also reflected the strength and dignity of the people who endured these conditions. "You see something in those faces that transcends misery," Roy Stryker said.[17]

About the same time these pictures were being shown across the country, articles about the dust bowl migrants were appearing in the press. John Steinbeck wrote a series of stories published originally in the *San Francisco News* in 1936 and later updated into an illustrated pamphlet, *Their Blood Is Strong*, in 1938. When he fictionalized the plight of the migrants in *The Grapes of Wrath* in 1939, the book caused a public sensation. Combining social and political commentary with artistry and emotion in the story of the Joads' migration westward, *The Grapes of Wrath* was not just the most important novel of the times but endured to become one of the greatest American novels. The timing of its publication was perfect to capture the

San Joaquin Valley pea field, the late 1940s.
From the album of Osie and Josephine Williams.

interest and enthusiasm of the public. People formed a picture of Okie migrants based on this book and the FSA photographs. They saw a group of people plagued by miserable conditions, lack of work, low wages, and the discrimination of the surrounding communities. They also saw a people with strength, compassion, and humor—all qualities that helped them survive the hardships of the times.

By the time *The Grapes of Wrath* appeared, the height of the Dust Bowl migration was past. The Los Angeles border patrol had turned back many migrants, who in turn warned others against attempting the migration to California. California also used a law that had been on the books since 1901 to claim that anyone bringing an indigent person into the state was guilty of a misdemeanor. These discriminatory measures served to keep the migration in check.

The Supreme Court ruled California's law against migrants to be unconstitutional in November 1941, but by then it was no longer a pressing issue. By 1941 California was more concerned about finding workers for the shipyards and defense plants that were springing up around Los Angeles and San Diego than they were about fending off a surplus of agricultural workers. The Okies were welcomed in California for the first time in 1941 and 1942 as they were absorbed into the booming defense industry. Their migration to the cities caused the first agricultural labor shortage since the Depression.

About the same time many Okies were leaving farmwork, in 1942 the U.S. Army demanded the removal of the Nisei (American citizens of Japanese descent) from more than half of Washington, Oregon, California, and the irrigated farmlands of Arizona. The uprooting of some hundred thousand persons, many of whom were farmers and farm laborers, intensified the demand for agricultural workers to such an extent that a wartime emergency program was initiated to recruit *braceros*—Mexican nationals imported temporarily to work under contract in the fields. By 1943, only four years after the appearance of *The Grapes of Wrath*, a California legislative committee was investigating the shortage of agricultural workers.

Although many Okies had moved to California cities to work and settle permanently, others had adapted to migratory life and returned to it in the postwar era. Many came to prefer it to a more settled existence. This process continues today: as some people "settle out," others choose to stay or even return to the migrant life.

"Seems like, a few years back, a lot of people were sayin' that they really had to get off the road, and most of them did," a picker told us. "So now, most everybody that picks fruit anymore does it because they really want to. They just find something in it that they can't give up."

The Okies who remained migratory in the 1940s and

1950s traveled between Arizona and California, working mainly in two crops: cotton and peas. For many old-timer migrants today, picking cotton holds a special meaning. It symbolizes their roots as migrants and creates a special bond between them: any genuine older picker will have picked cotton.

Picking in a cherry orchard in Washington, one picker calls to another, laughing, "Don't white boll my row! You're an old cotton picker, ain't you?" he asks, reassuring himself that his companion is familiar with the term. "Hey—it was the best thing for us pickers when they brought in those cotton-picking machines," he continues in jest. "We'd of been walkin' on all fours by now!"

Cotton-picking stories abound among pickers, affirming a sense of history within their own lives. Migrants who have picked cotton are often nostalgic about the fact that it was always easy to find work in the cotton in the 1940s and 1950s, wherever they traveled. It was the opposite of their experience in the late thirties, and they relished it.

"I remember when you could work anywhere. Wherever cotton grew, there was work. There was so much cotton it took thousands of people to pick it, and if you ever saw a cotton patch, you could just put on your sack and go out and pick it," recalled Dale. "I remember the first time my dad just went out to work and it wasn't that way. He thought the world must be coming to an end when a man couldn't just go out and work!"

Migrants tend to forget the brutality of the work, remembering humorous details. "I loved to pick cotton," Mattie told us. "The day before I had Esther, I picked nearly three hundred pounds of cotton. I'd been longing for a banana split for weeks, so bad, but we didn't have any money to speak of. So I said to Jay, 'If I pick three hundred pounds of cotton, then will you buy me a banana split?' and he said O.K. Well, I came just short of it, two hundred and ninety-something, but he bought me it anyway.

Boss man said if Jay hadn't of bought it, he would've bought it for me hisself!"

There are many conflicting memories of economics in the cotton-picking days. "We made more money picking cotton back then than we're makin' now," claimed Cecil. "And that was in the 1940s!"

But some people who were children in the 1940s retain strong images of poverty. "I remember one Christmas when we were picking cotton and we were real poor, and Daddy brought home a hundred-pound sack of beans and a hundred-pound sack of potatoes and said, 'That there's your Christmas present,'" Walter remembered.

His brother Daniel nodded. "Things were pretty bad back then, in the old days. When I was a kid, Ma and Pa would pick peas and I didn't even have shoes. I'd be out in those

"I'd be out in the fields and my feet would get so cold they were like clods in the dirt." Walter Williams, the late 1940s.
From the album of Osie and Josephine Williams.

fields and my feet would get so cold they were like clods in the dirt; they didn't seem like part of me."

Dale, who picked cotton later, had a strikingly different recollection. "I really have some good memories from that time," he recalled. "You could go anywhere and get a job, cotton grew all over and it was a long season. I used to pick cotton when I was a kid in California—around Tranquility. I would really pick that stuff—three, four hundred pounds. I'd work after school or on the weekend. You could make good money at it. That was '51 or '52 and I could make eight dollars after school—that was a lot of money back then.

"You'd go in and weigh your bags and they'd pay you right then," he continued. "Then they'd just get the change back 'cause you'd spend it on a soda or some food. They had a cookstand; you could get hamburgers or hot dogs. On a large crew, they'd have two or three cookstands. And they'd have

"Every time you'd go up with a bushel, they'd give you a big old half dollar and a dime." California, the late 1940s.
From the album of Osie and Josephine Williams.

Loading bushels of peas, California, the late 1940s.
From the album of Osie and Josephine Williams.

washtubs full of ice with soda pop. Boy, I'll never forget how an Orange Crush and a Baby Ruth tasted at about 10:30 in the morning!"

Migrant families who picked cotton and peas often lived thriftily and saved their money. They were proud of what money they'd earned. "Oh yes, we used to make good money," a picker remembered. "Twenty-five years ago when we was pickin' peas, they used to pay us sixty cents a bushel. Every time you'd go up with a bushel they'd give you a big old half dollar and a dime. Well, we used to just live off those dimes and save all the half dollars. After pea pickin' was over, we went up to a car lot and bought us a brand new car. We paid for the whole car in half dollars; that man was so irritated with us!"

Mattie also remembered saving money. "In three days, I

Family in a cherry orchard, California, the 1950s.
From the album of Osie and Josephine Williams.

picked enough cotton so I could go home to California and see my folks—I hadn't seen 'em in years. And Jay picked enough bolls to send me the money to come back."

In the late 1950s and early 1960s, the mechanization of agriculture and the increased use of braceros began to erode the few gains that American workers had made in agriculture. As the mechanical cotton picker gained wider use, thousands of migratory laborers were left without work. Pickers were desperate and raged furiously at the mechanization of cotton picking, but they had little recourse. "The pickers used to shoot at the machines—they hated them," recalled one old-timer.

"When they got the cotton machine, everybody had to have one," remembered Walter as he relaxed after working in the orchard all day. "A farmer would put his whole life savings, every last penny, toward gettin' one—they were really expensive machines. Then if it broke down, they wouldn't have enough

money to fix it with. Sometimes the pickers would throw spikes into that machine to make it break down so they could get a few days work until it was fixed. They were so desperate."

Walter's voice broke as he recalled that time. "When they brought those cotton machines in, they left thousands of people without anything. People who had a car and a trailer, who were doin' pretty well—I seen 'em walkin' out of Five Points, California.

"Those machines couldn't pick 'em with the leaves, so they had to have planes come and spray the cotton to defoliate them. And people would be out there in the fields picking a little bit of cotton, whatever they could get, and they would take it to the gin and get it weighed and get paid for it, enough so they wouldn't starve. They wouldn't say where it came from. And they would be out there picking and a plane would come by and just cut their heads off. One minute there'd be a man out there picking cotton and the next minute there'd be a man without a head. I've seen that. I lived through those days."

By the mid-1960s, when work in the cotton and the peas was no longer available, the Okies who were to remain in farm work made a shift to orchard work, picking fruits of every kind. They expanded their migratory routes to include citrus picking in Florida, Arizona, and California, and picking cherries, peaches, pears, and apples in California, Oregon, Washington, Montana, and Colorado.

With ladder work, the Okies found a new sense of dignity and a small measure of financial success. After a good season, a prudent worker was able to purchase a new car, a trailer, or a small piece of property in one of the southern states. Owning trailers to live in, and sometimes winter homes too, the Okies adapted themselves to the "fruit run."

The Okies discovered new territory in the Northwest, where orchards were smaller and there was a chance for real

relationships with small farmers. This difference from California agribusiness was true even in 1940, as John Blanchard describes in *Caravans to the Northwest*:

Between a considerable number of growers and their help, quite happy working relationships exist, despite the extremely low standard of living of the workers. This is because, in the Northwest, a majority of the growers are small owners. Dealings between them and their employers often are direct and on a personal basis. . . . This is in contrast to areas where farms are vast agricultural enterprises ("factories in the field") controlled by distant absentee owners or impersonalized corporations.[18]

Pres Wilson left Oklahoma in 1940 with his wife and nine children, and the family picked cotton in Arkansas, Mississippi, and California. In the late 1950s they began picking fruit in the Northwest, and they settled in a small town in Washington State, where they could make a living in the expanding orchard country. His daughter Gladys is old enough to remember what the change from row crops to orchard work was like for a child growing up with migrant parents: "I remember when we all worked together in the cotton. It was always so dusty. One time Ma made Jello and it was all covered with dust. Cotton was my worst experience. We had to travel from town to town. That's why us kids never got much education. But we settled down and didn't travel so much when we started picking apples and cherries. We could thin, prop, prune, and pick in the same area."

Her brother, Bill, also had fond memories of his family's move to Washington State to pick fruit. "We came out here to apple country in '58, '59," he said:

Left: *The Wilsons left the road for steady work in Washington orchards, April 1986.*

It was fun back then—everybody was family people. They'd be all these big families, a man and a woman and a bunch of kids. They were all nice. You didn't have to worry about anyone bird-dogging your row or anything like that. They'd give you a corner of the orchard and just leave you alone.

They just paid $3.50 or $4.00 a bin back then, but the apples were bigger and you could pick more bins. I could pick twelve bins and make fifty dollars—hell, that was a lot of money back then. You wouldn't have to work but a couple days a week if you didn't want to. There was always work in the orchard then—thinning, picking, picking up props—it went on a long time.

Part of the reason for choosing these fruit crops over row crops came from the domination of certain crops by braceros, Mexican nationals contracted to do farm labor in the United States. The bracero program had not ended with the wartime emergency. Braceros were favored by agribusiness. They came without their families and were expected to live in crude barracks. They were indentured for their transportation, and at any sign of dissent, they could be shipped back to Mexico.

Abuses had crept into the bracero system. Terrible living conditions, unsafe transportation, broken contracts, and the siphoning off of wages by unscrupulous labor contractors were some of the abuses that the Mexican government became sensitive to by 1951, when it urged the United States to enact laws to protect braceros. Under Public Law 78, an extension of the bracero program that was in effect from 1951 to 1964, the Department of Justice retained control over the admission and departure of Mexican workers, but the Department of Labor assumed responsibility for the recruitment and protection of the workers.[19] Minimum wages, standards of food and housing, and

Left: *Washington apples are the cream of the crop for pickers, Cashmere, Washington, 1973.*

other corrections to the former abuses were established. Ironically, these humanitarian protections had never been offered the American worker. The enforcement of the law, however, turned out to be token and perfunctory.

Public Law 78 was designed to be in effect for only two years, to tide agribusiness over another (though lesser) labor shortage because of the Korean War, but the agribusiness lobby was able to obtain extension after extension. The law specified that braceros were to be allowed only if sufficient domestic workers were unavailable, but agribusiness reversed the order. In effect, domestic workers were forced out of certain crops by the use of Mexican nationals.

At a Labor Department hearing in Los Angeles in 1962, James Davis of Sacramento told of his experience: "Right after the bracero program started I went to the growers I had known for years and I tried to get myself a job on the tomatoes, the way I always had before. I remember going to . . . one of the biggest growers in the area. He said, 'We're not using anybody but nationals this year.' That happened to me many, many times during those ten years."[20]

The use of braceros also artificially depressed the wage level. Another picker at the hearing in Los Angeles related, "I remember in 1948, when they didn't have any braceros, we got a dollar-ten a bucket [for cherries] then. . . . after they ran the nationals in, the price went down to eighty-five cents a bucket and even lower."[21]

Manuel Juarez of Stockton reported at the same hearing that conditions, as well as wages, had worsened:

In 1950 and 1951 we made pretty good money picking tomatoes . . . that was before they got the braceros in the San Joaquin County. After they got them the price went down.

They used to treat us like human beings. When I was planting strawberries over in the Salinas Valley, I remember they used to give us a ten-minute break every two and a half hours, morning and afternoon. No more breaks since the braceros. Water, same thing. . . . I guess they figure braceros don't need rest and don't need water.[22]

In *The Ground Is Our Table*, Steve Allen sums up the situation: "The Mexican contract-labor program was used to create a surplus of farm workers, thereby pressing wages down and compelling both domestic and foreign labor to accept substandard working conditions. . . . After deliberately lowering wages offered to American workers to a point where the employers knew they were not acceptable, the growers then offered the inevitable 'labor shortage' as the rationalization for importing Mexican nationals."[23]

The bracero program was always controversial. In 1964, after heated debates, Congress finally allowed Public Law 78 to expire. The expiration of the act had a dramatic effect in the employment of braceros. The number of braceros employed on California's farms dropped from 21 percent in 1964 to only 2 percent in 1965, and zero after 1967. (Some braceros were admitted under Public Law 414 between 1965 and 1967.)

One of the strong lobbyists against the bracero program was Cesar Chavez, who in 1962 had started the union that was to become United Farm Workers of America (UFW). The bracero program had been the bane of union organizers—attempts to organize them had failed and growers used them as strikebreakers. When the program ended, Chavez's organization began to grow, despite the increasing use of illegal aliens in farm work, a problem of another nature.

Because traditional strikes were not applicable to farm work, where work on each ranch was of such short duration, Chavez used the tactic of public boycotts to secure contracts. First boycotting products of specific large grape growers, by 1968 Cha-

vez had called for the boycott of all California table grapes. By 1970 the success of the boycott resulted in contracts with the grape growers of California. Shortly after this success, however, the Teamsters moved in, securing some contracts as well. Elections held under the short-lived state Agricultural Labor Relations Board in 1975 showed farm workers split about which union should represent them. But by the end of 1976 Chavez and the Teamsters had reached an agreement: UFW would have jurisdiction over primarily farming operations, while the Teamsters retained jurisdiction over canneries and food-processing plants.

The existence of the UFW had not significantly changed the lives of most migrant farmworkers, however. The farm workers in California's grape harvest were generally year-round, fulltime laborers who could find work within a couple-hundred-mile radius in the San Joaquin Valley. The majority of them were Mexican-Americans who identified with the ethnic bond of Chavez's "La Causa." For most of the Anglo workers, as well as workers with other ethnic backgrounds, the UFW was not the answer. Although some workers enjoyed working under UFW contract for awhile, the organization didn't really address the question of migratory laborers. Few migrants felt the effect of UFW's limited success.

At the same time union battles were being waged in the 1960s and 1970s, workers from Mexico (and later Central America) continued to flood into the United States in enormous numbers. Since the end of the bracero program, most of these workers were in the United States illegally. They needed the jobs that the Mexican economy could not provide, and even at low wages their American dollars held increased value in Mexico.

For their part, growers sought out the illegal aliens as workers. Unable or unwilling to make the transition to domestic workers after the bracero program died, growers were able to contract large numbers of illegals through "coyotes" who smug-

By the late 1980s, many of the Anglo workers who had persisted in agricultural work for decades felt themselves forced out by the sheer numbers of workers in agricultural work (and the consequent decline in wages). Under the Immigration Reform and Control Act of 1986, foreigners who could prove they had come to the United States and established residency before 1982 could apply to become lawful permanent residents. More lenient provisions for agricultural workers were offered in the Seasonal Agricultural Worker section of the act. Under this section, workers who could prove they had worked for ninety days harvesting crops in the United States between May 1985 and May 1986 were eligible to apply. Because of a waiting period before permanent resident status was awarded to these workers, those who applied were granted temporary status as of 1 December 1990 and then were required to go through another process in applying for permanent status.

Government sanctions against employers hiring undocumented workers were implemented at the same time as the amnesty provisions. All employees after November 1986 had to verify their legal status with valid documentation. Employers found in violation of the law could be fined for each offense.

Because the legal residency changes for foreign workers have been so recent and the sanctions against employers have rarely been enforced, it's difficult to evaluate the results of such measures on domestic farm workers. Because of the long history of foreign workers in agriculture, there are few domestic migrants farm workers left to carry on a traditional occupation. The wonder is that there are any.

"It seems like if you're an American and you've got white skin everybody thinks you should be elevating yourself to something better," one farm worker noted. "But we're stubborn, we won't do it! We want to keep picking fruit and tramping up and down the roads."

Mexican nationals largely replaced the Okies in Washington orchards by the late 1970s. Cashmere, Washington, 1976.

gled them across the border, or through Hispanic farm labor contractors. Because of their illegal status, these workers had none of the protection of the braceros and were unlikely to protest low wages or poor working conditions. The border patrol, mostly in California but in other western states as well, resumed their role of keeping foreign workers from settling in farm communities after the harvest was over. With the tremendous influx of illegal aliens, jobs for domestic workers became few and far between.

The advantages of migrant work and life are very real to the Okies who have chosen to remain in agriculture. Unlike most nine-to-five jobs, migrants can work with their families in a variety of job situations. They can obtain and quit jobs fairly easily and remain anonymous, relatively free of bureaucratic paperwork, applications, résumés, and taxes. This freedom to quit a job, collect your money, and move on has an appeal to the migrant that is in sharp contrast to the benefits of more stable jobs. It also contributes to the difficulty of organizing migrants. They prefer to deal with an employer on their own terms, independently of a group, and they nurture a basic distrust of organizations and unions. Okie migrants are more likely to leave than they are to initiate change in their working situation.

Perhaps because of their ease in adapting rather than organizing, Okie migrants lost many of their traditional work patterns by the late 1980s. The surplus of "undocumented" workers combined with the increase in mechanization have caused jobs to disappear. Child labor laws that prohibit families from working together, high gasoline prices, and low piece-rates have made it difficult for Okies to continue working at the few jobs that remain. "People have always undergone a certain amount of abuse in agriculture," a second-generation fruit picker observed. "But with the threat of replacement hanging over your head, there's very little you can do about it. So I think we tolerate worse conditions now than we ever have in history."

It's common to hear migrants say that this is their last year on the road, although they often feel a pull to return again. After a discouraging season, Bob felt sure he would not be back. "We've been picking for twenty-three years—this will be our last year. You can't make any money at it anymore and you can't hardly buy a job." Although he returned for a couple more seasons, eventually he made the difficult transition to a more stable life.

Many pickers have had to face the changes that are forcing them out of fruit picking. "I ain't missed a year in picking fruit in thirty-five years," said Pres Wilson. "It's been a good life for quite awhile, but it seems to be over now." His son agreed, "Most of the Okies and Arkies gave up a long time ago. There's not many places a white family can work anymore."

Despite the poor wages and conditions and the stigma of doing such work, there are still those who choose this life. The Okies who have stayed in farm work throughout the difficulties and hardships are more closely knit than the people who first came west out of the Dust Bowl. Large families often stay together to work in the orchard, strengthening their kinship ties through intermarriage between picker families. Their strong sense of family binds them to the work and way of life they love.

"Migrants in the past had a great pride, as they do now,"

Many Hispanic farm workers applied for legal U.S. residency, Madras, Oregon, 1977.

Walter Williams reflected. "Their pride was in their work and in trying to maintain a family life that would probably have been close to impossible without that type of work. And they did feel ashamed of it. But by the same token they had the shame, they also had the pride—and they bore the shame and lived with the pride. The pride was the thing that kept them goin' in the face of the shame they may have felt."

Fifty years after the Okies first migrated west to become part of the nation's agricultural labor force, a sturdy fraction of these still remain migrant, strengthened by their sense of pride and dignity in the work they perform and the way of life they lead. Bill's father left farm work for a job in the city but then felt the pull to return to a migrant way of life. Bill himself tried other occupations for years but found himself returning to fruit picking. He explains it all simply: "My father always said, 'It gets in your blood. It just gets in your blood.'"

Left: *Migrant culture is passed on to the young, Daniel and Lavonna Williams, Kennewick, Washington, 1975.*

I Always Keep Movin'
The Migrant Life and the Work

3. "Seems Like I'd Like to Hear Those Old Buick Tires Hum Again"
Following the Harvests

For Okie migrants, the harvest year begins in late April. That's when they congregate in Stockton and Lodi, California, to wait for the early cherries to ripen. They've traveled from Porterville and Bakersfield, California; Yuma, Arizona; or Lakeland, Florida, after picking citrus. Or they may have come from Oregon, Washington, Missouri, Texas, Oklahoma, or Arkansas—all likely places for a migrant to winter. Pickers pull their trucks, campers, and trailers into the camps a month early sometimes, anxiously anticipating the ripening of the earliest variety of cherries. Then they face another week or two of waiting without work until the cherry picking begins in earnest.

Left: *Dale Jones, Tri-Cities, Washington, 1977.*

Most migrants head south before the first snow, Wenatchee, Washington, November 1987.

For most migrants the winter has meant hard subsistence work in the citrus or scattered part-time work pruning for those who stay north, and the early spring often brings no work at all. The beginning of cherries promises work for the next five or six months, as the pickers travel north to follow the cherries and then pick prunes,* pears, and finally apples until mid-October. Soon there will be money enough for taking the family out for hamburgers and ice cream after work, for grocery money without degrading trips to the food-stamp office, and for gas for the truck to travel north. The kids will earn money for their candy, bikes, and new clothes.

Of all the fruits, pickers follow the cherries the most, traveling from California to Oregon, Washington, and Montana

*Pickers and growers in the Northwest refer to the small, blue-violet Italian plums as *prunes*. They are harvested for both the fresh and the dried fruit markets.

to keep up with the ripening fruit. Though individual jobs last only ten days to two weeks, a migrant can pick cherries over a two- to three-month period. But as the oversupply of labor has made jobs more scarce in the last few years, the gaps between jobs have lengthened, and an uneasy waiting in the migrant camps has become more common throughout the year. Migrants used to rely on the same jobs year after year, calling the growers ahead of time to let them know they were coming. But in the last five years more people have lost their old jobs and find them difficult if not impossible to replace with others.

Daniel and Darlene, a young couple from Texas with six children, used to go to Cove, Oregon, every year for a long cherry season. One year they found they had been replaced by tree-shaker machines (used only for fruit that will be processed). Dozens of their friends were also left without the jobs they relied on. Places on the cherry run where the Okies used to go every year—towns like Hood River and Salem, Oregon—became closed to them as a flood of undocumented workers from Mexico poured into these areas. Now the good money that the Anglo migrant once relied on in the height of the picking season is no longer there.

Sometimes a picker will replace a lost picking job with some other kind of agricultural work, but their preference is clearly with ladder work. We know of many pickers, ourselves included, who have taken work thinning when a cherry crop in an area has been damaged by rain or other bad weather conditions. But replacing orchard work with ground crops is more uncommon. One reason for this is a hierarchy in agricultural labor. Farm work has distinct categories of work, and Anglo workers tend to choose orchard work. The stoop labor of vegetable and berry picking is a last resort, and it is the least respected, even though it may be necessary at times to engage in it.

Indeed, many of the older Anglo fruit pickers grew up

picking crops such as cotton and peas, and they take much pride in relating stories of the past. "It's only recently that the row crops has gotten so separated from the ladder work," Walter Williams told us. "We used to pick peas in March and fruit all summer and pick cotton in the fall. The first time we picked cherries was in 1946. We picked them in a little place down in southern California, about a mile above the rest of the valley. Then we were picking peas and someone told my dad there were cherries up north, so we started goin' up north. The whole time, until after I married, we never did go out of California, because you could pick all year in California." He paused, then added, "And back in those days, you could only go so far with a Model T."

Planting trees, Chelan, Washington, 1981.

Anglo pickers specialized in fruit after the abundant supply of bracero labor began to dominate certain row crops in the 1950s. The fruit run is now an established though variable route that takes pickers to primarily orchard areas. Jobs in ground crops are rarely available, and the skills learned in fruit picking don't carry over into stoop labor. A few times Rick and I tried picking row crops with our friends the Williams when we had been out of work in the orchards for a long period of time. We tried onions, strawberries, and blackberries, all with disastrous financial results. Not only did we lack the requisite skills, but we missed the physical arrangements of orchards: trees and ladders meant shade, privacy, a view, and a more intimate sense of the work at hand—you didn't have the feeling that you were going down an endless row.

William Metzler, a sociologist with the U.S. Department of Agriculture, notes that "the stoop labor stigma has been associated largely with the Mexican laborers" and unfortunately this seems to be true—a carryover, perhaps from the days of the bracero program.[1] But the decisions to avoid stoop labor result from a variety of reasons that have little to do with race. As with any workers, farm workers are particular about the kind of work they do. Although they are liable to try anything in long periods of unemployment, fruit pickers are no more likely to seek out stoop labor than office workers are likely to try cherry picking.

People begin to follow the migratory fruit harvests for a variety of reasons. Many people are born into the fruit run: their parents did this when they were children, and they grew up with migrancy as a normal way of life. Others come to the work and way of life at some period of change or crisis in their lives. Fruit picking is accessible and equally available to all—no credentials or experience is needed to secure a job.

"I was born in the field, raised in a bin, and my folks figured when I climbed out of a bin I was ready to pick," joked Rob Wilson, a young man who returned to orchard work after a stint in the army, despite other job offers. "People always ask me why I work in the fields," he said. "They think people who work out here don't have anything else they can do. That's far from the truth."

Marty and Chuck began picking fruit after their marriage. "When we got married, we took our car and made the back seat into a bed and took off fruit tramping. Back in those days you just didn't *do* that kind of thing: it was a real sin to be a fruit tramp. Even now, our relatives would never just go off on a trip like us, with twenty dollars and no plans. I think they're envious of us really. It'd take them six months of planning to go this far."

Ross is an older picker who's always worked alone. "I

"When we got married, we took our car and made the back seat into a bed and took off fruit tramping." Peshastin, Washington, 1973.

started in the fruit in 1939," he recalled. "I was hobo-in' around. I got kicked off a train in Yuma, Arizona, and found a job pickin' grapefruit for three cents a box. I picked a hundred boxes and got three dollars. I was glad to have that three dollars too. Then I was in the war, out in the Pacific for four years. When I came back, I started pickin' fruit again. That was all I knew how to do except carry a gun, and nobody wanted you to do that."

Slim left Idaho to become a fruit picker after his wife died. "He used to be a real mountain man," said a friend of his. "He'd do logging for a living and live up in the mountains with his Indian wife and his twelve kids. Then after his wife died the welfare office wanted to take away his kids. They thought he couldn't handle all of them. So, he had a two-ton logging truck—he built a camper on the back of that, and they split. They've been working the road ever since." Most of Slim's twelve grown children have remained in orchard work.

"I used to work in Chicago in the factories," said Aristello, a Mexican-American farm worker. "When we moved west we started talking to people along the road, and they said you could make quick money picking fruit and have a lot of fun."

We've met people who came to migrant work after their families fell apart, after they burned out on high-stress jobs as professionals, or after they retired from other kinds of work. There are always people who pick fruit simply as a temporary means of making a wage without a long-term commitment. Often these people find advantages in fruit picking that a more traditional job doesn't offer. "Picking fruit is a pleasant way to make money," notes Jack McQuarrie in *Wildcrafting: Harvesting the Wilds for a Living.* "Its basic attraction is that it allows us to reconcile a love for travel with a need to work. Also we were working at our own speed and without a boss breathing down our necks every minute. . . . Especially enjoyable are those moments of peace and contentment when you pause to survey

East Wenatchee, Washington, 1982.

"I don't care anything about this fruit, but I like the people."
Kennewick, Washington, 1976.

the countryside from atop your ladder . . . from your crow's-nest you gaze over an ocean of fruit trees, stretching for miles in every direction."[2]

Most people who are picking fruit for just one season or are between other jobs or school don't think of themselves as fruit pickers. "I don't pick the fruit—I'm just doing it this year for something to do," said Jim, a former rodeo star. "I don't care anything about this fruit, but I like the people. If I was young again I'd never go near a horse—I'd follow the fruit run and contract some jobs."

But most of the people we worked with did consider themselves fruit pickers, even if they took other work in the winter. "We'll call ourselves fruit tramps—but only when we're joking. We're fruit pickers, not tramps," one picker asserted. These people have the pride of a craftsperson or a professional in their work and way of life.

Within this group of fruit pickers, there is much variance of the migratory lifestyle. For Troy and Betty, who both grew up picking fruit and have done no other kinds of work, following the harvests is the only way of life. They'll be in Stockton, California, for the beginning of cherries, then follow the harvests to Tri-Cities and Wenatchee, Washington, and on to Montana. Some years they come back to Wenatchee for the pear and apple harvests; other years they may pick blueberries in Michigan or apples in Colorado. In late October they make the long trek south for the orange harvest. There's not much money in citrus picking in Florida, so Troy and Betty contract small groves, picking and hauling oranges for the grower. Their two adolescent boys help them in the fields, seldom going to school. Their older daughter married another picker when she was sixteen. Troy and Betty and their sons live in a twenty-eight-foot trailer they pull from place to place with their pickup.

In contrast, Bob and Marlene and their four children don't move around nearly as much, although they pick fruit most of the year. In the winter they live in a trailer court in Porterville, California. They have a double-wide mobile home for the winter and a smaller trailer that they use for summer travel. During the winter, Marlene packs oranges and Bob picks when he can find work. Sometimes he finds other jobs for the winter, while the kids go to school. In May they go north about two hundred miles to Stockton. Then they follow the same route as Troy and Betty until fall. If they decide to stay north until the apple harvest, the children will usually start school in Wenatchee or Brewster, Washington, until they're ready to go back south.

Even for migrants like Bob and Marlene, who may not travel farther than an average American family on their summer vacation, driving and cars are of great importance. Cars and trucks are strong symbols to migrants—they represent mobility, independence, livelihood, and success. A shiny new Ford pickup is the migrants' status symbol. People identify with their vehicles, recognize each other by their rigs. "I didn't hardly recognize you—that's a different rig you're driving this year, ain't it?" an acquaintance will say.

Car maintenance and repair are major concerns to a migrant, whose work depends on being in the right place at the right time. There's nothing worse than being stranded on the road on your way to a job, with no money to repair the car. Mechanical skills are almost a necessity. It's not uncommon to see an engine being rebuilt in a migrant camp, with many of the male pickers volunteering their time to help. The lack of time and money forces migrants to develop a great resourcefulness that has its roots in the Depression.

Right: *"We'll call ourselves fruit tramps, but only when we're joking. We're fruit pickers, not tramps." Cashmere, Washington, 1982.*

People like to reminisce about those times when life was harder but also simpler. "You know, back in the early days of cars, they were real simple machines," Paul told us one day, as he looked up from the complex V-8 engine of his Chrysler, "and when something went wrong, you'd just try to fix it yourself. Like if you threw a rod on an old car, you'd just go get you some bacon rind—in those days everybody ate bacon with a big old rind on it. You'd just wrap the bacon rind around the crank shaft and bolt on the rod, and that bacon rind would act as an insert. It sounds funny but it worked! " Paul leaned against the fender. "Another thing we used to do, if you got a hole in your radiator, is just pour a can of condensed milk down there, and it won't clog up neither. 'Course, I wouldn't recommend it except in an emergency—but you have a lot of emergencies in Arkansas!"

Migrants have a way of surviving those hard times on the road with a blend of courage, patience, and humor that comes from having been there before. "We had a bad flat tire once 'bout twenty years back," recalled Mattie. "We was in Indio right next to some colored peoples' backyard. That was the worst flat tire we've ever had—we set there for a night, the whole next day, and part of the next night tryin' to get it fixed—tryin' to use a pole for a jack and it kept breaking. Jay, he never would go ask those people for help, I guess he thought he was real independent or something, so I finally went over there and borrowed a jack.

"Walter, Jr., was a baby then, and he was cryin' for milk. All in the world we had was thirty-five cents, and milk was twenty-five cents a quart then, so I went over to the store to buy him a quart of milk, but on the way I stopped and put a dime in the phone and called my mother and asked her to wire me twelve dollars.

"We went to the employment office, and they said there was absolutely nothing, but maybe, *maybe*, we could get work in a few days picking dates down south. We was driving down there

Car repair at the orchard camp, Lodi, California, 1980.

and it was right around Thanksgiving, and we didn't have a thing to eat, but we went by a carrot field and we stole some carrots. Somehow, Jay had got a dollar then and I went to the store and bought some ham hocks and we cooked them with those carrots and that was our Thanksgiving dinner. It sure tasted good!"

Those kind of hard times still exist for some people. I remember once when we were camped in a park in Milton-Freewater, Oregon, waiting for the prunes to ripen. A family in a station wagon drove in, and the driver asked some of the other pickers if there was any work available. He shook his head when he heard the answer. They were broke, he said, and hadn't been able to find work in weeks. He casually listed some of the car troubles he'd had, but he shrugged good-humoredly about his situation. "I guess we'll go on down the road," he said. "They're gonna need some hands to pick all this fruit one of these days."

Earlier that summer, in Wenatchee Heights, we'd met another family who lived in their station wagon. As we drove to work every morning at daybreak, we'd see the car by the road where they'd spent the night. The luggage racks on the top of the old station wagon were loaded down with mattresses, boxes, and tires, reminiscent of the Okie jalopies of the 1930s and 1940s. When we met the family, they were complaining about the lack of steady work here. "I've gone a hundred and ten thousand miles in this car," said the man. His leathery face showed the wear of hard work and travel. As he talked, his wife gave the children packaged doughnuts and milk for their breakfast, and they sat on the hood of the car to eat them. "I've picked apples in Illinois and New York and the Carolinas, peaches in Georgia, oranges in Florida, cherries in California and here. I'm going to Oregon now—we can't make any money here."

Fruit pickers generally live close to the edge financially, and they talk about their near-poverty with wry humor. In a cherry orchard one day when dark clouds threatened rain, one picker yelled out, "I sure hope it don't rain—I'm broke!"

Another picker answered him, "Well, the weather don't care if you're broke or not. I been broke before and it rained on me anyway."

"I got a solution to that," said a third picker. "I'm foldin' my money in half and sleepin' on it to see if I can double it."

A migrant's automatic response to poverty and hard times is to leave in search of greener pastures. For a fruit picker, to have wheels is to have hope. "Like my father always said, 'I wouldn't own anything that didn't have wheels on it!'" Walter, a second-generation picker told us. Not only are cars, trucks, and trailers the most major purchases a picker will make, they are a constant source of conversation and speculation. Buying, selling, and trading take up a large amount of the migrants' leisure time. Fruit pickers are frequently preoccupied with trading cars,

"I guess we'll go on down the road. They're gonna need some hands to pick all this fruit one of these days." East Wenatchee, Washington, 1982.

Right: *"I've gone a hundred and ten thousand miles in this car." Wenatchee Heights, Washington, 1974.*

campers, and trailers. For many of them the activity has the status of a second job, involving them in a continual cycle of looking for good deals, trading, fixing up, and selling vehicles and homes on wheels.

The actual time spent driving to the next job is also disproportionately significant, a time that migrants love to talk

about, a time when they feel the most free. Although it may be lonely, boring, or worrisome at the time, travel time is prime raw material for stories and conversations later.

After a job is over, people rush to hook up their trailers and cash their checks before the banks close, to get their *white-line money* and hit the road right away, even though their next job may not start for a week or two. They're anxious to leave an area once the fruit is picked and they have no real reason to be there anymore. Farther north, in another orchard area, there is at least the prospect of work, and if the weather cooperates, there may be work right away.

"When we move, we move fast!" Burt told us proudly. We made it from Stockton to Tri-Cities in less than eight hours. I drove that '55 Chevy—you know, that car moves! My wife drove the GTO and we raced all the way up 97. I'd cut her off and keep ahead of her through those curves, but she could take me on the straightaways. She's a helluva driver! We went right to work that morning, picking cherries in Pasco."

Though migrants usually travel in single-family units, occasionally we have traveled together with other pickers. Once we caravaned from Stockton, California, to Tri-Cities, Washington, with seven other cars, most of them pulling trailers. We drove down Interstate 5 through California, stopping to wait for each other at the rest areas. When we stopped for the night at a park just across the Oregon border, the children ran off their excess energy while the adults sat around together until midnight telling stories of other trips. The next day we traveled beautiful U.S. 97 through isolated pine forests and rolling farm country. We stopped at a state park near Bend, Oregon, to see the ice caves that had been carved out by lava long ago. When we came back from seeing the caves, Mattie invited us into their trailer for a home-cooked meal of meatloaf and mashed potatoes, corn, biscuits, and salad. Then we drove on, across the

"I wouldn't own anything that didn't have wheels on it." East Wenatchee, Washington, 1980.

border to Washington, and camped at Hat Rock, by the Columbia River.

Many migrant camping spots are little-known places where they can camp for free without being harassed. But that's not always the case, as Mattie told us. "Once we were camped here, and Darlene and I were right in the middle of making a big batch of blackberry jam when a cop came along and said, 'You people will have to leave here immediately!' We said, 'But Officer, can't we just finish making this jam?' He said, 'I'll give you ten minutes and if you're not out of here, I'm taking you all in to the station.' So we had to just leave our jam making in the middle, hook up our trailers, and go!"

But even with our conspicuous group of trailers, we weren't bothered that night. When our group drove into Kennewick the next morning, several people met us at Columbia Park. Walter and Daniel's brother Paul and his family had left Texas at the same time we left California and had beat us there. Our friends Bill and Vicki drove up, pulling their shiny Airstream trailer. They'd left California the night before and had driven nonstop to Kennewick.

Traveling together we experienced strength and security

"He was used to the traveling life and moving all the time; he couldn't set still." Eastland, Texas, 1970.

as well as companionship. If one vehicle had a flat tire or an overheated engine, there was plenty of help available. But as successful as the migrant caravan was, it was not repeated. Usually migrants are too individualistic to coordinate their traveling styles with others. But however they travel, migrants share a love of travel that at times seems almost like an addiction.

When we lived in Texas one winter with our migrant friends Walter and Mattie Williams, the talk often turned to traveling and the desire to begin the seasonal fruit run again. We'd known the Williams family since we'd worked in the citrus in Florida, years before. Their six children were young then, and despite the poverty and hard work they'd known, the family had a strong spirit. Walter had grown up picking fruit, after his father left Texas and taken his family to California in the Dust Bowl days. Now Walter was committed to making migratory labor something to be proud of. After traveling and working in the harvests for twenty years, he had finally bought a barren plot of land in Texas and a mobile home to come home to after the harvest each year.

One cold March evening, as the winds buffeted the thin walls of the mobile home, Mattie was describing to us Walter Jay's insatiable urge to travel. "Now I was raised in California," she told us, "and the furthest south I ever went was Riverside, California, and the furthest north I ever went was Eureka, California. But Jay, he was used to the traveling life and moving all the time—he couldn't set still. He'd get the blues every once in a while and he'd have to go get in the car and he'd just drive, four, five hundred miles. Then he'd come back and he'd be all right for a few more months. Even now he still gets the blues. He was just saying the other day he wisht it was time for the cherries again."

Walter nodded his head in agreement. "One of the worst times to be driving is when you've been driving all night and the sun comes up and hits you right in the eyes. You'd think that of all the times you'd like to remember about goin' down the road, that wouldn't be one of them. But sometimes, when I'd been on one job for a few months and I'd get the itch to drive, I'd just drive east all day with the sun coming up, and then turn around and drive back with the sun goin' down."

Listening to Walter I was reminded of another migrant we'd met the summer before, while picking prunes in Oregon. Joanna was a vibrant, middle-aged woman who lived with her husband and three children in a tiny sixteen-foot trailer. While she worked, she sang country-western love songs, her loud clear voice ringing through the orchard. On one of the many days in between work, she sat outside her trailer on a campstool. Clad in a long pink robe, her dark hair let down to her shoulders, she stirred a pot of bubbling blackberry jam over a Coleman stove.

We talked with her about the migratory life, and she looked back on her days of real nomadism with nostalgia. "From the time I was pregnant with my first son until he was two months old, we traveled thirty thousand miles—I mean, we moved! I love to travel, but my kids hate it with a passion. They hate to transfer schools; they like the schools in Arkansas. But when all my kids get growed, then I'll do as I like. I got too much Gypsy in my blood to stay in one place too long."

It's common for migrants to control their impulse to move somewhat during the years their children are in school, then to increase their mobility again. If they've worked another job and have saved some money, they may get a fancy new trailer or motor home to go back on the road in style. We know many older, "retired" people who come back after a long absence to pick fruit, enjoying both the added income and the sociability of their particular migrant circuit.

Some pickers manage to travel without their own vehicles. The hobos we've met who travel to the orchards by rail are the classic *fruit tramps*. Unconstrained by families, they are

Stockton, California, 1974.

continually on the move. As one old hobo picker told us, "Well you got to travel! What do they expect you to do—sit home and watch TV? I know I'm going to have some fun while I'm alive!"

Okla Slim, who edits a newsletter called *The Hobo*, writes nostalgically about friends who have "caught the westbound": "They die alone, in the Jungle or in a boxcar and yet in the midst of the only friends they have, the other Bo's. They have held on to a little freedom to the last."[3]

Most of the migrants we worked with were *rubber tramps*—migrants with their own vehicles. Often they would take "steady work" in the winter but their nomadic instincts called them back to the road in spring, when cherries are ripening. "I haven't missed a cherry run in thirty years," proclaimed Bill, wiping the sweat from his brow after a long day of work. Although Bill has proved himself capable in other kinds of work,

he's most proud of being a fruit picker. "I almost missed one once when I tried to settle down and be like everybody else," he continued.

I had a job once for eighteen months, at the American Pipe Company, building the tunnel under the bay [Oakland] for that metro system. But it drove me nuts—I drank all the time and I had to get away. I'd take off Friday and not come back till Monday. I wouldn't even stay with my family. I thought I'd settle down—that's what everybody thought I should be doin', working a steady job with a steady income. I had all kinds of things on the time plan—car, house. But I hated every minute of it. And I almost missed the cherry run, but luckily the union had a strike. God, was I glad! I just loaded up the car, set those old tires humming! That's something Dale's father always used to say, about tires humming. I can just see him out there in the cotton patch, and suddenly he looks up and says, "Seems like I'd like to hear those old Buick tires hum again."

Left: *"Well, you got to travel. What do they expect you to do—sit home and watch TV?" Leavenworth, Washington, 1974.*

4. "We Can't Be No Worse Off Than We Are Now with No Job"
Looking for Work, Waiting for Work

In late April, the early variety of cherries in the orchards around Stockton, California, begins to turn from pale green to reddish-pink, and the roads are full of pickers looking for work. Often migrant fruit pickers return, like migratory birds, to the orchards where they have worked every spring for years. For those pickers who find themselves without a job to return to, there are days ahead of driving back roads looking for work, talking to growers, contractors, and other pickers for leads or connections to a job.

Even for those lucky enough to have an annual job to come to, there may be a long period of waiting before the work actually begins. In a journal I kept years ago, I described the situation of waiting for work in a migrant camp:

27 May
Arriving in Lodi yesterday to a full camp. Everything seems much the same as last year—the old crew with a few new additions. Some of the people have new rigs—usually larger or

Stockton, California, 1976.

Left: *Blossom thinning and pollen picking begin in early spring. Crescent Bar, Washington, 1980.*

newer trailers and trucks. The kids have grown bigger. The ground is still that dusty burnt ash. The smoky dust blows into the trailers, turns the children coal gray, and covers everything with a film of dirt.

It's hot here, in the nineties, but the evening breeze and the shade of a few tall trees make it more tolerable.

We expected the mood of the camp to be dismal. Almost everyone has been camping here for a month or a month and a half, yet there's been only half a day of work. The early cherries were rained out. Now we're waiting for the late cherries to start—a rather hopeless prospect also. Most of the blossoms came off in the rain, leaving hardly any cherries on the trees. As if that weren't bad enough, we have a bigger-than-average crew. Soft-hearted Otis has let on a lot of extra people—friends and relatives of the crew. He planned on needing them in the early cherries but since that fell through they've all waited for the late cherries.

A combination of desperation and excitement pervades the camp full of pickers waiting for the job to begin. Each day of waiting is filled with anxiety and anticipation but little activity. There's not much to do in the surrounding community that doesn't involve spending money, and money is in short supply for migrants this time of year. They've spent what they have in travel, and they may have gone for months without work. Consequently this time of waiting becomes a time to socialize with other pickers in the camp, and the focus of the conversation is often speculation about the crop.

Among Okie migrants, it's the men who seem to have more time to socialize, while the women—in traditional roles—cook, clean, shop, and watch the children. Men especially tend to define the limbo time of waiting with a particular ritual each morning.

After early breakfasts, men drift out of their trailers, coffee cups or cigarettes in hand. The trailers are parked close together on a cleared patch of land surrounded by orchard. The dirt road through the orchard borders the migrant camp on one side. The men walk casually across the road to the orchard, greeting each other with a nod of the head. "Mornin', Otis. Ya think we're ever goin' to get ta pick this fruit?"

The men form a small circle on the edge of the orchard. There are six or seven of them, their ages ranging from twenty-five to sixty. Rick and I hang back along the edge of the circle, listening and occasionally participating. Although I am conspicuously the only woman in the group, the men take little notice of me. They examine the unripe fruit carefully, placing clusters of the small pale cherries in their hands, discussing their condition minutely, as if they could will them to ripen sooner. "They still look pretty green to me. I reckon it's ten days away," Otis comments. "Well, now I wisht I'd stayed in Arizona. There ain't much goin' on there, but at least I could make enough to buy groceries."

One of the younger men leans against the trunk of a tree. He has the look of another time: his face is pale and narrow, with a long forehead and deep-set hazel eyes, topped by a shock of blond curls. Striped overalls and a worn work shirt cover his thin body. "Well, you know a fruit tramp," he grins, hooking his thumbs in his overall pockets. "When he decides to go, he's gone! We'd be pickin' oranges down there in Porterville, and someone'd say, 'Cherries are a good four weeks off, no use in goin' up north.' Next mornin' they'd change their mind and they'd be gone. Sometimes they'd go up there for a day and turn right around and come back, and then go up there again. Yeah, about six weeks before the cherries start, there's no tellin' what will happen!"

"It's funny," agrees another, addressing his explanation to Rick. "We only pick cherries about forty days a year, but we call ourselves cherry pickers."

"Well, you know a fruit tramp. When he decides to go, he's gone!"
Shorty, East Wenatchee, Washington, 1978.

"The cherries is all there is now." A stocky man squats near the ground, drawing lines in the dust with a twig. "If you don't make it in the cherries, you ain't gonna make it. Though there's some that make it in the apples too. But you can't hit it in the cherries and then try to make the same kind of money in the prunes and peaches and apples and oranges all through the year. If you did, you'd be dead by the time you were twenty-five!"

"Well, we make pretty good in the cherries," another man says. "But by the time you figure there's eight people working, and the whole rest of the year when we can't make that much, I doubt if I make more'n twenty dollars a day."

"I ain't too sure we're goin' to make it at all this year," the young man in overalls says wryly. "We might just be standin' around the welfare office if they don't ripen up here real quick. You know, they say there's only a dime's difference between the man that works and the man that don't work—and the one that don't work is the one with the dime!"

As everyone chuckles at that last line, a truck pulls up beside the group and the grower, a young man with a tanned face, leans his head out of the window. One of the older pickers takes a few steps out of the group to talk with him. "They're still awful green. Just not ripening up in this cool weather," the picker says, shaking his head.

"Yeah, I'm hoping we don't get any more rain now," comments the grower. "I reckon they're ten days off. Well, the field man will be out Wednesday to let us know. The grower waves goodbye and the truck ambles down the orchard road.

The men stand around a little awkwardly, their ostensible purpose of evaluating the cherries now gone. Then they start to disperse, making excuses as they move away. "Well, I guess I should see if Marge is ready to go into town," says one. "Yeah, I got to look at that truck of mine. That starter's been actin' up," says another. They seem disheartened as they walk back across the road. They know there won't be any work for at least ten days, and there's nothing to do but wait. The cherries won't be ripe up north for weeks to come. But often there are other jobs in the area if one has the patience and persistence to pursue them.

Going to search for a job can be a time-consuming and discouraging task. "Come back around five A.M. on Thursday and I'll see if I can put you on," a grower is apt to say. "If some of my pickers don't show up, I'll have a ladder for you." Pickers who really want the job must rise early, get ready for the day's work and drive—often ten miles or more. More often than not they will be told, "Sorry, I'm full up."

Before most pickers will even ask about a job they will spend many hours and gallons of gas driving around checking out the orchards. They're looking for large cherries, trees loaded with fruit, and trees spaced apart so their limbs aren't tangled together. Preferably, the trees are well pruned and a picker can reach all the cherries with a ten- or twelve-foot ladder.

Often a group of relatives or friends camped out together at a pickers' camp will go look for another job together. Since they may come to an orchard camp weeks before the work there is scheduled to begin, they need other work to fill in the time.

One time when we were staying in a migrant camp with about a week before our next job was to start we set out with several other pickers to look for another job. Like them, we couldn't miss days of possible work during the short-lived cherry season. Ruby, an older woman, had said she could use her "connection" to a grower to get us all jobs. But before we committed ourselves to asking for a job, we wanted to check out the orchard surreptitiously to be sure that we could all do well there. Crammed into a car with six other people, we drove several miles down back roads lined with orchards, until Ruby directed us to turn down a dirt driveway. We stopped in the middle of the orchard. The orchard was quiet—the cherries weren't quite ripe enough for picking so no one else was there. We swung open the four car doors and got out to congregate for a few minutes under the closest tree.

"Man, these trees are really loaded!" exclaimed Walter. His brother Daniel chewed thoughtfully on a cherry. "They sure are roped on there alright." The men drifted off to another tree, picking up branches to feel how heavily they were set with cherries and eating an occasional cherry to assess its size and ripeness.

Meanwhile the women remained near the car. Darlene scrutinized the first tree with the observant eye of experience.

"They're loaded alright, but look at the size of 'em. I bet a lot of these cherries won't even make twelve-row!" she said critically.

Ruby agreed. "There ain't nothin' worse than pickin' those little cherries. You pick and pick and your bucket never does seem to get full!"

The men returned, meandering through the orchard investigating a clump of cherries carefully. "There's some pretty loaded trees out there," Daniel concluded. "It looks like a good job to me."

The women disagreed. "You know how those little cherries just pack down in your bucket," Darlene reminded us.

Walter interrupted, saying "Let's just go on up there after awhile and ask about it. We can't be no worse off than we are now, with no job." Despite the pickers' attempt to be selective and discerning when looking for a job, the bottom line was often what was available when they badly needed a job. Because the best money is in the cherries and then in the apples, there is intense pressure to work every available day during these harvests. There is plenty of dead time in between harvests and in the winters—pickers want to insure that they have a minimum of days off during the harvests.

Besides driving around to look for work, pickers usually call ahead to a farmer they have worked for to confirm their next job. They also rely on the grapevine—word-of-mouth reports of crop conditions and jobs, which are often completely without truth. One year a rumor circulated that our next job up north—a job that many people were counting on to make the bulk of their

Right: *They say there's only a dime's difference between the man that works and the man that don't work—and the one that don't work is the one with the dime!" Rodeo Slim, Finley Point, Montana, 1982.*

Far Right: *Lambert cherries, Stemilt Hill, Washington, 1978.*

money in the cherries—would not be hiring any of us. The rumor was that the farmer had fired the contractor and had hired a whole crew of "wetbacks." Everyone was upset about the possibility and the rumor persisted for several days until phone calls were made to the grower, who denied the rumor.

The spread of false rumors about crop conditions is also commonplace. "I hear that hailstorm in the Tri-Cities wiped out the whole crop." "They say the trees are so loaded up in Brewster that one person can make eighty dollars by noon." These are examples of both negative and positive rumors we've heard about crops. Often such reports have a grain of truth in them but are very exaggerated. If a picker tells you about a bumper crop, it's likely that it's a good crop although it may not be as good as you were led to believe. Similarly, impressive stories about how much money a picker made a day picking cherries are usually misleading. Although such stories can be true, they usually represent one long day of incredibly hard effort by an experienced picker in the best fruit. Pickers realize the distortions such stories can lead to, but they take pride in their picking skills and want to tell about their abilities. Unfortunately, farmers often use these unrepresentative high figures to try to prove that pickers are making plenty of money—in their view, too much.

Exaggerations or distortions also occur about the length of a job and when it will begin. If a picker says it's a ten-day job, it usually lasts a week; a week-long job is usually finished in five days. If picking is supposed to start Tuesday, more often than not it will be Wednesday or Thursday before it actually begins.

Pickers can also be misled by farmers and contractors, who rely on field men for the go-ahead to begin picking. They may be told that a job will begin on a certain date and even leave one job early to travel to the next one, only to have to wait for days before the work begins.

Even under the best circumstances, when a picker has secured and begun a good job, there are irritating delays, layoffs because of rain or unripeness of a variety of fruit (for example, in the same cherry orchard, Bings, Lamberts, Vans, and other varieties will ripen at staggered times). A typical work record I kept during a ten-day period at a cherry orchard in Kennewick, Washington, illustrates this frustrating fact of agricultural work:

June 8—Worked 5 A.M. to 2:30 P.M., averaged 4 boxes a tree.
June 9—Got laid off at 1:00.
June 10—Rained out at 10:00.
June 11—Laid off.

Driving around the orchards looking for a job, Brewster, Washington, 1977.

June 12—Laid off.
June 13—Got a good set after half a day, 5 A.M.–2:30 P.M.
June 14—Doing pretty good but he called us out at 1:00 P.M.!
June 15—Finally made our $100! 5 A.M.—3 P.M.
June 16—Again! Started in Vans about noon.
June 17—Took until 1:30 to finish. Windy and dusty!

The record shows that within the ten days we spent on the job, we had only four full days of work. Of course, even on the three days that we had to quit at one o'clock, we had already put in eight hours of work, but we didn't consider that a full day of work in the cherries. Because of the long days during the cherry harvest and the pressure to make most of our money then, we needed to work nine or ten hours to "make our quota." That quota, which may differ from picker to picker and job to job, is a personal expectation of how many boxes will be picked each day. Countless factors can erode such expectations. Because rain causes picked cherries to rot in the box, pickers are called out of the orchard in anything more than a light drizzle. Moving to other sections of the orchard, finishing one variety of cherries and starting another takes large chunks of the pickers' time, for which they are not compensated. Finally, bad trees—ones with too few cherries or cherries that don't come off easily; or ones with unpruned or tangled limbs—can cause pickers to not meet their quotas.

But in spite of all the frustrations, delays, and disappointments, there is nothing so satisfying to a picker as a good day of fruit picking. It's a rare day when the weather is perfect, not too cool or too hot, and a promising row of loaded trees stretches out ahead. The camaraderie of the crew is pleasant and the boxes of cherries seem to fill almost effortlessly with plump fruit. These days are rare even in the best harvest, but they are always what a picker hopes for at the beginning of the fruit run and remembers long after the last fruit of the season is picked.

5. "Are Ya Gettin' Rich?"
A Work Day in the Orchard

It's the first day of the cherry picking season, the day we've all been anxiously awaiting. The alarm blares at 3:45 A.M., shattering my peaceful sleep. I reach out to stifle it and rise automatically. Sleepily, I flip on the small kitchen light in the trailer and put water in the kettle for coffee, then splash some water on my face to help me wake up.

Outside the window a silvery moon shines in the indigo blue sky. The lights of other trailers blink on in the dark, and through the trailers' screened kitchen windows, I see women's hands at their sinks and stoves. Through the thin walls of the trailers parked side by side, I hear their voices as they wake their husbands and children. "It's nearly four, Travis. Get on up now!" "C'mon Paul, it's already gettin' light." The pungent aroma of

Left: *Montana Lamberts, Flathead Lake, Montana, 1975.*

bacon fills the air as the women fry it for the family breakfast, often to be eaten in the field during morning break.

I wake Rick and pour cups of the brewed coffee to sip while we get ready for the day. Then I pack our breakfast, lunch, and snacks into bags and pour the rest of the hot coffee into a thermos. We dress in layers of clothes. The summer morning is chilly, but we know we will be hot and sweaty in just our T-shirts by ten o'clock.

There are rosy shards of light in the sky now, as morning approaches. The sounds of dogs barking and buckets clanging mingle with voices and footsteps outside our trailer. People are on their way to the orchard already at 4:30 A.M., and those who aren't ready to go yet are at a disadvantage. Hurriedly I gather the other essentials for our day in the orchard: a watch, some gloves for the cold morning, adhesive tape to wind around our fingers to protect them from tearing on the rough bark of the trees, a water jug. Clothes, toys, and a blanket for Zak, our toddler. All this, plus our food, is piled high in our cherry buckets and backpacks. Bundling our sleeping son in a blanket, we walk outside, our cherry buckets swinging heavily from a strap across our shoulders. Far ahead of us, other pickers walk on the dew-dampened path to the orchard.

The pace increases to a near run as the pickers approach a group of ladders in the middle of the orchard road. Forming a Stonehenge-like circle, aluminum ladders of varying sizes gleam in the early morning light. The pickers scrutinize the ladders quickly, with a sharp eye for size and brand name. In front of us, a picker pulls out a ten-foot ladder and lifts it to check its weight. He rapidly pushes out the tongue of the ladder, testing to see that it swings freely and balances well. Satisfied, he swings the ladder over his shoulder and hurries off through the orchard.

We select ladders and wait for Otis, the contractor, to direct us to our trees. Otis, normally slow paced and relaxed, is

Getting lined out on a row at five A.M., Benton City, Washington, 1977.

Right: *Kennewick, Washington, 1975.*

now rushing about the orchard *lining out* the pickers—showing them to their trees. "Here, I'll do that," he says, taking my ladder from me courteously and carrying it down the road. He leads us to our *set*—a group of trees that we are to pick. We look over our four trees and grumble about them as we unload our buckets and lay a blanket on the ground for Zakary.

Instinctively, we look around us to see if anyone else has a noticeably better set. "Well, that tree over there sure is loaded. And wouldn't you know, the Matthews got it!"

The beginning of a job invites much speculation about the first set you'll receive. Everyone has had ample opportunity in the previous days to look over the orchard, knowing where the crew will begin to pick. On that basis, people decide whether to rush out at the crack of dawn to try to get the first set, or to linger over their coffee a little longer in hopes of reaching a better section of the orchard. On some jobs this tension is avoided by having the pickers draw numbers for their first set the night before. Then everyone knows just where they'll start the next morning. Without this system, there is always the possibility for *bird-dogging*.

At work in the orchard, there are constantly suspicions of favoritism by the contractor as well as accusations of *bird-dogging*. *Bird-dogging* is the name for a number of crafty methods of sniffing out the better trees in the orchard and figuring ways around the impartial system of distributing trees to the pickers. Sometimes pickers take unusually long coffee breaks to avoid an undesirable set of trees coming up—if they wait long enough, other pickers will come along to take the bad trees. In other instances of bird-dogging, pickers will leave one person behind to finish up a set while the rest of the family moves ahead to a good upcoming set. Sometimes children are used to scout out the good trees ahead, and occasionally they will *bottom* them, picking the fruit on the bottom of the tree. Since nobody wants to pick a bottomed tree, they will effectively lay claim to the tree. The practice of bottoming trees is frowned upon, however and pickers caught doing it are apt to be fired from a job. Other methods of bird-dogging are more subtle and difficult to prove.

Some pickers feel that being aware of how good the trees are in each part of the orchard is a necessary job skill, and that waiting for good trees to come up is a legitimate form of bird-dogging. And there are a few people who make bird-dogging a regular practice, buttering up contractors and farmers to insure that they're given the best of the crops to pick.

When we began picking fruit, we were shocked that fruit pickers, at the bottom of the social ladder, would cheat on one another at work. Walter tried to explain it to us. "To expect migrant workers to live with dishonesty all their lives and then be honest in return is a pretty far-fetched idea," he reflected. "If you plant a bean in the ground, you'll more'n likely get a bean at harvest time, and honesty is something that just wasn't planted from the very beginning. It's been a dog-eat-dog world and most of the fruit pickers will cheat on one another in the field."

In general bird-dogging is talked about even more than it is practiced, and pickers are quick to accuse someone who took a longer coffee break or got an exceptionally good tree. Calling someone a bird-dogger is an insult, if done seriously. Calling someone a bird-dogger in jest, however, is one of the most common jokes heard in the orchard.

As we swing our ladders into the cherry tree and climb up, we see Al and June walking by Earl's set, carrying their ladders. "Hey Earl," calls Al, "how'd you bird-dog that tree? Otis really gave you a good one there!"

"Well, the tree's pretty good," quips Earl. "There just ain't no cherries on it!"

For our first job of the season, this crop is disappointingly light. A late frost in California this year has wiped out much of the cherry crop here. There are few cherries where there should be thick clumps, and they are scattered throughout the tree, so we have to take our ladders all around the tree to get them. It all amounts to more work for less money, but everyone is trying to stay in a good humor this first morning.

Black Wenatchee Bings, Wenatchee Heights, Washington.

People continually walk past us down the row to a new set. Because the sets are so thin, it doesn't take a family long to pick them. A set of four or six trees may yield only two to eight boxes this year; on a good year it might yield forty.

This dismal situation seems to demand humorous banter to lift our spirits. Pickers project their voices so they will carry through the thick foliage and span the distance between the sets. In this way, everyone can laugh at the jokes and participate in the conversation.

Al, a hefty man with a deep, low voice, calls out to Earl, "I told June she could go out and work 'til one or two o'clock and then I'd come out and work 'til one-thirty or two-thirty, but she wouldn't go for that. I don't know why."

Earl chuckles and calls back in his strangely high voice, "I tell you, I'm gonna make a lot of money next winter so if they have another crop like this, I don't have to be out here picking it!"

Otis, walking down the row, hears the dissatisfaction behind the comments, but laughs with them. He's the contractor for this job, but he's a picker too, the rest of the season. It's not uncommon for a picker to run one job of the season—organizing the crew, hauling ladders and boxes, conferring with the grower, and picking when he gets the chance. His wife also picks during the day and does the book work at night, recording how many boxes each picker totals each day.

Otis is a solidly rounded man of about fifty, dressed every day in a crisp cowboy shirt and new blue jeans. His voice is soft and unhurried. "Well, everytime I get all moneyed up and don't want to work, I go over to Tahoe and lose it all. Then I can work real good again for awhile!"

As I listen, my hands rustle the leaves of the trees, searching for cherries hidden under them. When I find a branch hanging with cherries, I tuck it under my arm, leaving both hands free to bend back the stems on the clusters of cherries. Done correctly, they drop off easily, and I carry the clusters to my metal bucket. The first cherries in the bucket make a ringing sound against the metal, like rain drumming into a pail. When everyone starts to work in the early morning, it is that sound that breaks the stillness—plink, plink, plink. The sound of the cherries grows softer as the bucket fills.

I climb down to move my ladder, and the ladder tongue clangs against the steps as I pull it toward me. Holding the ladder upright, a few inches off the ground, I move it to the next set in the tree and swing the tongue in toward the center of the tree. A space in the tree for the ladder to go is also called a *set*, and a good pruner will think of making these sets for pickers to have easy access to the fruit.

With my bucket about one-third full, I climb to the top of the ladder and begin picking again, working my way down the ladder, cleaning the nearby branches of all the cherries as I go. My bucket full, I pick out the leaves and spurs from the top and

Picking out the leaves, Kennewick, Washington, 1976.

No fruit is left behind. Okanogan, Washington, 1978.

Right: *Benton City, Washington, 1976.*

toss them on the ground. The *spur*, a woody part just above the stem, is not supposed to be picked because it produces the next year's fruit, but inevitably everyone gets a few. Before we started picking cherries, our friend Shorty warned us about getting too many spurs. "Just pull 'em off and put 'em in your pocket," he cautioned. "Don't let the boss catch you with spurs in your bucket!"

Not too clear on what the spur actually was, we assumed it was a tiny bit on the end of each stem and laboriously tried to pull the stems free of this bit. How do you pick these things anyway? we wondered, as we watched other pickers' stacks of boxes pile up while we still worked on our first box. Finally we asked our friend Walter who was working near us, and he showed us what the spur really was. He laughed, "When I was a boy, we were working in a cherry orchard and my dad would pick all the spurs off the cherries in his box and give them to me to go throw over the fence. Well, a man came up to me and said, 'What are you doing, little boy?' and I said, 'My dad told me to throw the spurs over here so he wouldn't get in trouble with the

boss.' The man said, 'Well, I am the boss!' That man fired the lot of us then, and that was the last time my dad ever did that."

We soon learned the importance of clean picking—no spurs, no stem pulls, no broken limbs on the tree. Pickers stake their reputations on this. "One thing I can say, at least I don't have a reputation for picking rough," an older picker told us. "I've always made sure to fill my boxes and pick them clean."

In contrast a rough picker may be fired from jobs if he or she doesn't respond to warnings from the grower or checker (a person designated to check boxes of fruit for spurs, bruising, or other problems). Pickers with reputations for hard picking as well as hard living may be known as *Stockton pickers*, a term to describe the people who managed to pick the huge, sparsely fruited trees of Stockton. Some of the large extended families described as *Stockton pickers* have been picking fruit for generations and are almost legendary for their speed as well as their style. And though most pickers like to pride themselves on the quality of their work on a good job, a poor job with low wages will bring forth the opposite emotion. Then people will often boast about the amount of stem pulls or spurs in their boxes as a small act of revenge toward the farmer who cheats them out of decent wages.

Now, as I dump my full bucket into the box, I consider how far we've come from the days when we didn't even know what a spur was. The ladder work is usually easy now, where once it inspired fear, frustration, and painstaking effort. After years of picking, I can shoot the ladder tongue through the tree to the right distance, climb with ease to the top step to reach for the cherries, move the ladder out from under the branches and around the tree, and carry it to the next tree effortlessly. There is a pleasure in carrying out the task with a minimum of movements, quickly and efficiently. At the end of the day, I'll be tired from the heat, the constant motion, and the strain of carrying the

fruit, but now I don't think of that. Now I only want to fill the next bucket, the next box—to finish my tree and my set and move on .

As we work on our last tree of the set, Slim walks by. One of the few people working alone on this crew, his name describes his tall, bony body. He walks with his shoulders slightly hunched over and his head bent under the large straw cowboy hat he always wears. We say hello and he stops for a moment to chat.

"Well, these cherries don't fill up the boxes very quick, do they?" comments Rick.

"No, you can't hardly find the cherries for the trees," Slim drawls. "Hell, I done picked two trees by myself and got 'em both

"You can't hardly find the cherries for the trees!" Kennewick, Washington, 1974.

in one hand!" He ambles down the row, his ladder under his arm, his bucket, filled with only a thermos and a paper lunch bag, slung on the other shoulder.

We finish our first set of four trees and collect our belongings, yelling the pickers' call for a new set, "Timber!"

"Over here!" Otis yells out to us. "Down the next drive." A drive is where the truck or tractor drives between the rows of trees.

As we walk down the row, people call out to us. "Hey, it's about time you got down here to the good stuff! Don't you take that tree I got my eye on now!"

When we reach the last person working on the row, we look around at the next trees. We have our choice of the set on either side of the row, but they both look so bad there's not much difference. Otis walks by and says, " Well, you got a choice. Two sorry trees or three sorry ones." We throw the ladder tongues into the trees on one side of the row. Earl and his family have finished their set just after us, and they follow behind us, carrying their ladders. Rick jokes, "Well, Earl, I saved you a good one."

"You really did it to me this time!" Earl exclaims. In mock anger, he pulls a spur off some cherries and throws it under our tree. We all laugh.

By now our son, Zak, has woken up from his morning nap, so we all sit down for our coffee break—breakfast. Buckets turned upside down are our chairs, and the wooden boxes are turned over and put together to fashion a table. We spread out bread, peanut butter, yogurt, and cereal. The steaming cups of coffee warm us in the cool summer morning.

Across the row from us on the opposite set, Griff and Billie sit down for their break, taking cellophane-wrapped doughnuts and a thermos of coffee out of a zippered plastic carry-bag. Griff, in his midsixties, has a weathered, friendly face and thinning gray hair under his baseball cap. Billie is a large woman, her face shaded by the scarf and sunhat she wears. Smiling or scowling, she expresses her emotions strongly, both physically and verbally. "I don't take no guff," she says about herself, and she's been known to walk off a job in a hurry if she suspects favoritism or unfair practices.

As we eat our breakfasts, we chat with Griff and Billie about the picking. A picker strolls down the row past us, carrying his ladder to a new set. "Can't get rich eating!" he calls out. "We're not gettin' rich anyway, so we might just as well eat!" we respond. "I can make more money by accident than I can in these damn cherries," Griff adds.

A young girl follows the picker and stops to play with Zak. Zak leaps up from the cherry box, spilling his cup of cocoa. We clean it up and go back to work while Zak and his friend are still occupied with games in the dirt.

This is a good working time, the chill of the morning abating as the sun gets higher in the sky. We're warmed and stimulated by the food and coffee in our bodies. We pull off our sweaters and slip the straps of the cherry harness over our long-sleeved shirts. I look at my watch so I can time how long it takes me to fill a bucket. Then I try to pick faster to beat the original time. Sometimes Rick and I try to add incentive by competing against each other: we keep our stacks of boxes separate, seeing who can pick more. Usually we pick at the same speed so the competitive idea doesn't work. We work equally, both of us picking top to bottom on the tree. On a large tree, we begin with our ladders next to each other and then circle the tree in opposite directions. On smaller trees, we'll each pick the whole tree by ourselves. But some couples separate the work more: men picking tops and difficult inside branches, women picking bottoms and middles of the tree on shorter ladders.

Pickers are always aware of how fast everyone else is picking. Griff and Billie, across the row from us, pick about the same amount as we do, but they're twenty-five years older and have slowed down somewhat. Most of the pickers who have grown up in this kind of work can easily out-pick us. The piece-rate system rewards speed rather than amount of time spent, and the competition between the pickers can be intense.

Although each picker determines the speed at which he or she picks, the social pressure to compete with other pickers is intense. There are frequent questions from co-workers about how much you have picked that day and constant comparisons to other workers. Embarrassment about their picking speed causes many slow pickers to try to work faster.

As I walk to the outhouse, I observe high stacks beside the sets and mentally calculate how much faster someone else is picking and how many more boxes their trees have produced. The people moving ladders, dumping cherries in boxes, and writing tickets to place on top of the stacks have lean southern faces, strong bodies, and swiftly moving hands. Walking down the row, I have glimpses into their work days too. A man runs up a ladder and there is a thunderous sound as the cherries drop into his bucket. A child sleeps under a tree, her mouth open in relaxation. Another man smokes a cigarette, one leg propped up on the ladder, his bucket, half filled with cherries, still on his shoulders. A big Mexican family works together, the children climbing the tree noisily with homemade buckets of coffee cans and tupperware. Their mother, her head swathed in a pale green turban cloth, moves very slowly, an island of calm in a turbulent sea of activity.

Near the outhouse two older children talk to each other. "How many boxes d'ya have?" they ask. "Only three, but I was helpin' my ma." They savor their few idle moments. One of them teases, "I'm gonna tell your dad you were foolin' around up here." "Naw . . ."

The inside of the outhouse smells of cigarette smoke. It's

Above and Right: *Pickers keep a quick and steady pace, placing their ladders with precision. Cashmere, Washington, 1974.*

clean now, except for the flies, but in a few days it will be dirty, filled with excrement, the toilet paper long gone. Even on jobs where chemical toilets are used, the cleaning schedule is seldom adequate for the intensive use of the whole crew.

On my walk back, I see other scenes of pickers in various stages of work. One young couple picks frantically, while their toddler wails at her imprisonment inside a playpen. Two teenagers steal a moment of flirting, their hands still occupied with cherry picking as they work with their families on nearby sets. A blond woman sits on her bucket, holding a small baby. Family life

coexists with the work, and each becomes an integral part of the other, a reality that rarely exists in the United States today, where work usually separates parents from their children and each other.

Back at work, I too am involved in family life, watching my son, loosely monitoring his play with other children, going up and down my ladder to get him what he needs. Sometimes he picks a few cherries from the bottom in a little coffee-can bucket, but usually he plays with toys, cherry boxes, sticks, and dirt; climbs trees; and finds birds' nests, spiders, or bugs to investigate.

After our next move, about 11:30, Mike and Joyce, other friends, call out to us, "Ya'll had lunch yet?" We bring our thermos and bags of food over to the tree where they are sitting with two other large families. We try to find a patch of shade; it is hot now. Upside-down cherry boxes and buckets are arranged between several trees by the children. The women mix tuna or ham spread, and the children pull dozens of slices of bread out of the bag. The men, some of them lying comfortably in the dirt, talk about the work and tell stories.

The lunch is consumed in an atmosphere of chaos as kids fight over cokes and chips. Someone looks for a spoon; a child is sent to the car for the forgotten can-opener. The toddlers stumble around the boxes, their faces covered with cherry juice and dirt, as their mothers try to feed them. A month-old baby lies in a baby bed sucking a bottle; an older girl leans over the bed and coos to her. Two older boys wrestle in the dust; the teenagers exchange shy, flirtatious comments across the impromptu table.

Coffee and cookies follow the sandwiches. Then Mike gets up. "Well, I reckon I better get back to work now or I may not be able to get up." Everyone boos at him. "What's your hurry? Nobody's gonna take those cherries away from you!"

Joyce says, "I ain't goin' back to work yet. You can just jump up by yourself. Anyway, I ain't feelin' so good. I may go in early today."

"I ain't feelin' so good neither, since I seen my last set," jokes Mattie.

Despite the comments, everyone begins packing up the remnants of food, gathering the garbage, stacking up the cherry boxes, and putting their cherry buckets on again. The lunch break has been less than half an hour, but everyone feels obliged to get back to work soon. When the crop is bad, no one can afford to sit still for long. And when it's good, no one wants to miss out on the good money. Although there is no time clock to punch and no schedule to follow, people generally limit themselves to two short breaks a day, though a few people seem to take countless small cigarette or coffee breaks without missing a beat in their picking. A picker working solo will often work straight through, with only the shortest of breaks for a gulp of coffee or a sandwich hastily eaten while leaning against a ladder.

Pickers treasure the freedom of not having to punch a time clock, but their own work ethic and unspoken rules (and those of growers as well) are often as strict as the regulations they despise. If it is light enough to pick by 5:15 A.M., then everyone is expected to be in the field by 5:30. Someone arriving at 6:00 or 6:30 A.M. is considered a straggler. If they come at 7:00 or 8:00 A.M., they may be out of a job—or at the very least they will have acquired a bad reputation. People who choose to come and go as they please, take breaks as often as they like, and even drink beer on their breaks—all within the confines of the piece-rate

"Gettin' rich?" Benton City, Washington, 1976.

Family lunch is quick and chaotic. Kennewick, Washington, 1976.

system—will be stigmatized for such choices. They are usually denied the better jobs and are forced to work on jobs with tall, scrappy trees, even if their picking skills are equal to those of pickers on a good job.

After lunch, the heaviness of food in my stomach and the rising heat of the day combine to make me feel drowsy.

Moving to another set, Pasco, Washington, 1977.

All of a sudden the picking seems monotonous and irritatingly slow. Pickers walk past us, uttering comments I know I will hear thousands of times before the season is over. They're stock phrases for pickers: "Gettin' rich?" "Made your hundred yet?" "Hot enough for ya?" "Are ya gettin' 'em?" To the last, we respond as always, "I think they're gettin' me!"

The flatbed truck comes down the row, and men jump off the back to load the boxes on. A checker takes the perforated half of our ticket for the number of boxes, leaving us with the other half for our records. The grower is with them this time, looking at the cherries, both for ripeness and for picking quality—the boxes should be level full, cherries should have stems but not spurs, most of the leaves should be picked out, and the cherries should not be bruised or crushed.

The grower chats with the pickers. "How're ya doin' today Mike?" "Alright, but they sure are light this year, ain't they?"

"How's it goin', Griff?" "Well, I hear it's supposed to hit the dollar mark by this afternoon." The grower laughs. "We may have to call you out in a bit. I heard on the radio it's supposed to reach a hundred today."

In the afternoon heat, beads of sweat roll down our faces, and we drink all the water we've brought for the day. The cherries are getting soft from the heat, making them fall off their stems too easily. Picking cherries without stems is called *milking*. It's sometimes done on purpose for processing use when the cherries can't be sold fresh, but on most jobs when the cherries are milking, or *shelling*, easily, it's time to stop picking for the day. The cherry-picking day usually ends by two o'clock because of the heat. In cool weather, pickers may work until three or four; on extremely hot days they may be called out of the field at noon or one o'clock.

At one o'clock, we try to make our one last effort of the day, knowing that we have only an hour of work left and calculating how little we've made. "Oh, well, it's just the first day," we rationalize, knowing that the rest of the orchard is no better. The piece-rate system gives you the feeling that you're racing against time, and the work day goes rapidly.

At two o'clock Otis walks through the orchard, calling, "Fill 'em up!"

"How much do you lack?" the pickers call out to others in their family as they work together on filling the boxes. Fifteen or twenty minutes later, most people have filled their boxes, and we collect our belongings one last time and straggle back to the camp.

Cove, Oregon, 1978.

"How many didja get?" pickers ask each other as they walk back to the camp. A few people stand or sit around the camp talking after work, but most retreat to their trailers to shower, if they are lucky enough to have one, or simply to rest. The work day is over, and even though there are still six or seven hours of daylight left, most of those hours will be spent recuperating from this day and preparing for the next.

If We Don't Like It We Can
Go down the Road
The Bosses

6. "Ain't Nobody Owns Me"
Pickers and Growers

On a hot and sweaty afternoon in an orchard in Lodi, Cali-fornia, we worked with other pickers on a section of trees located behind the grower's house. From the perch of our ladders, we could look over the high fence into the backyard of the house, where a large pool was being put in. The loud, grating noises of cement trucks and workmen obscured the more delicate sounds of cherries dropping into our metal buckets. In the sticky heat, the noise served as an irritating reminder of the sharp contrast between our own low wages and our boss's wealth.

"Wish he'd hurry up and get that pool done so I could take a dip," commented Mabel, wiping the sweat from her brow. "From here, I could just dive off my ladder and get cooled down real fast."

Left: *Polk City, Florida, 1975.*

"If we don't like it, we can go down the road." Marty, Cashmere, Washington, 1974.

When we sat down to take a break with a few other pickers, more resentments against the grower surfaced. Even though this farmer had a friendly rapport and a longstanding relationship with most of the pickers, in the last several years tensions had begun to build. This year, with a poor crop and a drop in the wages, pickers were particularly discontented. When the grower walked through the orchard earlier that morning to pick up the boxes, Rick had asked him: "How come you're paying so low? We got paid more than that five years ago, and we've picked all your worst crops." The grower shrugged. "Well, it seems the only reason is that everyone else is doing it."

"Bud's just like the rest of 'em—they all know they can get away with it," Mabel told us cynically, after we'd related the incident. "They all get together before we ever pick a cherry and decide what they're gonna pay the pickers. We don't have no say in it whatever. If we don't like it, we can go down the road."

Another bone of contention among pickers was that the annual end-of-harvest party had been canceled this year. Every year we'd worked there, Bud had given the pickers a wonderful party at the end of harvest. He grilled steaks and provided plenty of food and drinks on the patio outside his home. All the pickers came with their families to socialize with his family and enjoy the rewards of a job well done. Pickers appreciated the effort and expense and the way it reflected his appreciation of their work. The fact that there was no party this year symbolized for them a change in that attitude.

"Well, it looks like we ain't gonna get no party this year. It's the first year I can recall that Bud's done us that a way," grumbled Cecil, an older man with bright blue eyes deeply set in a face hardened with wrinkles. He poured himself a cup of coffee from the thermos. "It's on account of that pool, y'know. All that party money is goin' into building the dang thing."

Mabel scowled. "Yeah, and the worst of it is, he ain't raised our wages in three years, but the gas and the groceries keeps goin' up just the same. I'd a lot rather had me another

Right: *Bill Wilson picks a few tunes at the end of harvest. Cashmere, Washington, 1980.*

Harvest party, Cashmere, Washington, 1980.

"You think they need you and me out there? They don't need us."
Wenatchee, Washington, 1977.

quarter a box and ferget the party!" Mabel took a couple cookies from the cellophane package she'd put on the ground in the center of the group and shifted her bulky body into a more comfortable position.

"Well, we ain't gonna get either one," commented Leroy, Mabel's slim husband. "You know, I used to think Bud was the best guy in these parts to work for, one of a kind. He'd come up under your tree and talk with you real friendly. But this year, he smiles and all, but he won't hardly come around 'cause he knows the pickers is mad. And you know good and well, ain't nothin' we can do to change his mind."

The fact is that pickers aren't valued as much as they were ten or twenty years ago. The last twenty years have seen a huge increase in the numbers of immigrants, legal and illegal, who are willing to accept low-paid agricultural work as an entrée to the United States. As in the days of the Dust Bowl, too many people competing for agricultural jobs has created a situation of advantage for the grower.

The Okie pickers, who have known better days and have committed their lives to this work, find themselves again with no power or control—pushed out of their chosen occupation.

They'll try to hang on to this work as long as they can by working for the few growers who still employ Anglos. But any talk of a strike or concerted action on their part dies quickly—they know they have no real muscle.

"Naw, he'd have him a crew of Meskins out here so fast, he'd never have to stop loading boxes," said Cecil, after we mentioned the possibility of a strike.

"If we could just get everybody together to talk to him, maybe we would get a raise, suggested Geraldine, Cecil's wife. She was a slight woman with a face as wrinkled as her husband's and dry, bleached hair pulled under a bandana.

"That's a hard thing to do, get people together," said Cecil. "They can get those Meskins cheap, but y'know one of these days all those Meskins are gonna sit down on 'em, and that price will go up to four dollars a box. Now the Americans won't do that. You can talk to 'em about a strike and they'll say 'sure' but you can't get 'em to stop working."

"That's right," said Leroy. "You think they need you and me out here? They don't need us. This farmer's just like the other ones. One phone call and he can have a whole different crew out here in the mornin'. My brother-in-law Jim was workin' a job last year and they kept stringin' him along, pickin' all the scrap, and as soon as they got to the good stuff they fired the whole crew. Had a new crew out there in the mornin'. I seen it happen over and over again."

As the relationship of pickers to growers has changed, the nature of the work has changed accordingly. Only a few years ago, when the pickers felt Bud was their friend and ally, when they were treated with the respect of equals and consulted about their knowledge of weather and crops, their attitudes were very different. They saw themselves as working together with Bud to accomplish the task of harvesting the cherries at the peak of ripeness, at the time when he could get the highest price. They believed they would reap some of the benefits of his economic success.

But now that they're no longer consulted or treated as equals, now that they're simply a labor force, they've lost much of their ambition and concern for Bud's welfare. They leave work early rather than suffer through the heat for pay that everyone knows is too low. This situation seems to deteriorate every year. Older farmers who developed relationships of mutual respect with the pickers sell their orchards or pass them to their sons, who often have more modern ideas of "labor management."

"They just don't treat you like a real person," said Daniel as we talked about how relationships with growers had changed. "I saw that farmer welcome Jay the other day—I couldn't hardly believe it. That's the first time I've seen a farmer welcome a picker—in, oh, at least twenty years. I used to go up to those farmers and introduce myself, try to shake hands, but I don't do that anymore. I got tired of being rebuffed. The grower would say, 'That's okay, I can get your social security number later,' and it was insulting. They didn't want to meet me as a person, just wanted my number."

Most old-timers remember a situation of mutual interdependence with growers that made them feel more valued than they do today. A picker who made the long trek from Washington State to Montana only to find that the cherries had been ruined by rain blamed the difference in attitude on the oversupply of workers, "Well, it useta be we'd come up here and they'd just guarantee us a place to stay and two, three hundred dollars even if the cherries was all busted, just so a guy didn't lose nothin'. But now you know they got these Meskins workin' out there and they stopped doin' that."

Darlene agreed. "People can go out there and work for years and years for the same farmer and be just as loyal as they can about picking his good and his bad, workin' for whatever

Bob Malloy, Walla Walla, Washington, 1977.

wages result in lowered standards of quality. There is more than one way to pick fruit, and pickers compensate for lower wages and alienation with greater speed and less care in the picking.

The discrepancy between the way growers live and the way pickers live is another ever-present theme in the relationship between pickers and growers. Because pickers working in smaller orchards are often near a grower's home or in contact with the grower as they work, they are very aware of the gap between their incomes.

"It gets to me the way these farmers are always cryin' about how they don't make nothin'," a picker I met at the food bank in Wenatchee complained, echoing what I'd heard countless times from pickers in the fields. "Anytime they say they've had a real bad year, they'll be drivin' brand new cars or buyin' new tractors or motor homes. They don't count that. They say the pickers are the only ones makin' any money, but you don't see the pickers drivin' new cars every year!"

"Hell no!" agreed his companion. "They see us with our motor homes or trailers and think we're doin' just great, but those ain't our vacation homes—that's what we live and work in year-round. Half the time they ain't paid for anyway."

Despite these discrepancies, a rare grower with the insight to treat pickers decently can benefit from the relationship. One grower who insisted on careful picking of his easily damaged cherries paid pickers above the going rate. "Some growers might think it's too much," he said, "but I'm making money and the pickers are getting a bonus. I think it really gives me a lot more quality."[1] Growers like this one, although they are few and far between, elicit long-lasting loyalty on the part of pickers. Often there is a close, personal relationship between pickers and such growers, nurtured by continued concern about their lives as well as their crops.

Another farsighted grower, who outlined her techniques

price he wants to pay and everything, thinking that he'll treat them right, and then all of a sudden you go out there one year and he's got all wetbacks out there, tellin' you he don't need you anymore. Well, that's the kind of loyalty the farmers give you, if it means another dollar in *their* pocket. They couldn't care less about who they got pickin' or who's been loyal to them and all."

The loss of mutual loyalty and concern results in an irreparable rift between workers and growers. The increasing alienation of pickers makes their work less efficient, and lower

for "personnel management" in the magazine *Good Fruit Grower* pointed out that "you get what you pay for." She provides a complex of housing, complete with furniture, bedding, and kitchen items. "I firmly believe if you give someone a nice, clean comfortable place to live, it will be the same when they leave," she writes. "Respect means treating people who work for you as you would like to be treated." She demands quality work and pays incentives in order to get it. She socializes with the pickers at the end of each day, offering them beer and pop. "I have a harvest party in my home, complete with food, dancing, and

Tempers can flare at payoff time. Milton-Freewater, Oregon, 1977.

kids. I invite my people to some of the parties I hold in my home. They invite me to theirs—and I go."[2]

This grower claims to treat the pickers as equals, but her constant reference to them as "my people" is typical of the old-fashioned paternalistic approach where workers are treated as children. "I have found that my people rise to my expectations," she writes.[3]

Although this approach is preferable to the disinterested, impersonal style of agribusiness, it is still objectionable to pickers sensitive to the implications of paternalism. "I hate for a boss to say '*my* pickers,'" explained Randy, a young man who was raised picking fruit. "Just like sayin' 'my niggers.' That might have gone on a hundred years back when they had slaves, but those times are gone, man! Ain't nobody owns me—I ain't *his* picker!"

Unequal power is characteristic of any employer-employee relationship, but the difference with migrants is that they see themselves as independent because they don't work for any one employer. In the past, when jobs were more readily available, pickers felt that they could choose which employers to work for—a factor that made the balance of power more even. Pickers often tell stories that reverse the traditional relationship with employers. The story Travis told one evening to a group of pickers in an orchard camp is illustrative:

Well, I was working for that guy Dean, up in Brewster, and he's a pretty good guy to work for. I liked him—he'd come up and talk to you just like he was a picker. So one day I was asking him, "How do you work this job anyway? Do you hire the same people year after year?" He said, "No—there's a lot of people I don't want to hire the next year. So what I do is, when there's a picker I don't like, I just put a little black mark next to his name."

Well, I got to thinking about this, and the longer I thought about it, the less I liked it. So at the end of the job when I went to

86 / The Bosses

get my check, I says to him, "Remember a few days ago, when you told me that when you don't like a picker you put a black mark next to his name? Well, when I don't like a grower, I put a black mark next to his name so I remember not to work for him again!" That guy has thought a lot of me since I told him that— or at least I think he has!

Even the underlying tensions implied in the story are outweighed by the feeling of mutual respect. Growers and

End of harvest, Okanogan, Washington, 1978.

Left: *"We're just so durned independent, and it's an independent way of makin' a living." Walter Williams, Okanogan, Washington, 1978.*

pickers share a stubborn sense of their own independence. "We're just so durned independent," our friend Walter explained. "And it's an independent way of makin' a livin'."

Unfortunately, the large influx of workers in agriculture has made migrants more dependent on growers, and Okie pickers, who can no longer rely on a list of good growers to work for, must accept their devalued role or leave the work altogether.

With the current trend toward agribusiness, the traditional loyalty and respect that pickers and growers once accorded one another seem particularly outmoded. Not so long ago end-of-harvest parties were the norm, as pickers and growers celebrated their joint success in completing the harvest. Now such parties are a rarity. The growers' personal relationships with pickers have eroded as individuals and families are replaced by crews organized under contractors. Pickers are no longer consulted about their opinions, as growers come to depend on the "field man" to give specialized information about the crop. And small farmers, pressured by increasing governmental regulations and paperwork, are hard-pressed to find the time to socialize with the pickers as they used to.

Growers and pickers still depend on one another but more often it is in an impersonal, nameless way. If small farmers lose their footing in American agriculture, the human element of working in the fields will be lost as well.

7. "It Seemed Like We Owed Him Something and We Didn't Owe Him Nothin'"
Pickers and Contractors

"Maybe someday the relations between pickers and growers will be better—but I don't think so," John commented after our third day of work picking cherries in an orchard in Stockton, California. We'd just learned what price we were being paid for our work.

Since the first day we started picking, we'd asked both the contractor and the farmer the price, but we could never get a straight answer. "He hasn't told me yet," the contractor said, "but I reckon he'll pay about three dollars." The grower said,

Left: Contractor takes a short break on a long day. Kennewick, Washington, 1976.

"I'm gonna call some of the other guys and see what they're paying."

Most of the other pickers didn't even ask what they were getting paid. It seemed as if there were an unwritten law prohibiting such direct means of finding out your wages. "I imagine he'll pay us what we got last year," one picker said. "Al says they're payin' three dollars across the road—I 'spect he'll pay the same here," said another.

On the third day, Otis, the contractor, came out to the field to talk to the pickers. He looked embarrassed. "He says two dollars a box is all he'll pay," he told us. "I tried to get him up, but he won't budge."

The pickers were furious. "We've been coming here for eight years and we've picked some of the worst crops for him. I never thought he'd do us that-a-way!"

We'd expected a slight drop in wages from last year, when the crop was so poor that the pickers had to be compensated somehow. Even at $3.50 a box last year no one had made much money. But we'd been paid more than two dollars a box even on his last good crop, three years ago, when gas and food were less expensive too. Now the price was so low we would barely pay for our travel expenses to get to California. "I can't hardly believe it," said one of our picker friends as we ate our lunch in the fields together. His wife shrugged as she fed her baby a spoonful of cereal. "Well, we'll make enough to get to Washington, and we'll make good money up there."

Rick and I found it more difficult to reconcile ourselves to the price drop, so after work we went to talk to Otis. His trailer was parked on the far end of the camp. "Oh, c'mon in," he said when he saw us. "She'll be right back," he said to me, referring to his wife. "She went to talk to the women." He offered us some coffee, and we sat down on the trailer couch. Because we'd known Otis as a fellow picker as well as a contractor, we were on

"He says two dollars a box is all he'll pay." Kennewick, Washington, 1976.

friendly social terms with him. But we couldn't restrain our anger at the terms we had unknowingly been working under.

Otis shook his head. "I know none of 'em's too happy about it, but there ain't nothin' in the world that I can do about it."

"But he paid more than that on his last good crop, three years ago!" we protested.

"I know it," he said. "It's not much more'n half of what we got last year. But that's all the farmers are payin' them Mexicans and they've got him thinkin' that that's all he should pay too."

Later we confronted the grower and he confirmed what Otis had told us. We had a choice: we could go back to work at that price or we could quit.

Years ago there might have been another option. Dissatisfied pickers would have gone to the contractor as an organized group to demand a higher wage. They would have threatened to quit together. The contractor would have relayed the message to the grower, negotiating for the pickers.

Now it was clear that the pickers were too powerless to risk the security of their job. They trusted certain growers to pay them fairly and when that trust was broken, their only recourse was to hope to make more money on the next job or to find another job in the area the next year. In previous years, even if an organized protest had not been successful, at least several pickers would have quit. But this year, no one believed it would do any good to protest, and no one quit. They grumbled at first but worked on, accepting the drop in their wages.

The contractor in this situation was as powerless as the pickers, and his dual responsibilities only caused him problems. Though he tried to advocate for the pickers whom he identified with, and was one of, his word carried no real weight behind it. He too had to accept the grower's final decision and try to keep the pickers from getting too upset.

A contractor is employed by the grower to run the picking operation. He or she receives about 12 to 15 percent of the total payroll, though it is often calculated by the box, bin, pound or work-hour. The contractor's job may include driving tractor or supervising tractor drivers, supervising the picking crew and organizing the order of the picking, loading and hauling boxes (or overseeing a crew that does this) and getting them to a packing plant or a site in the orchard where they are picked up, and recording the work and paying the workers.

The role of the contractor varies in different crops and regions. In Florida, it's common for people to actually contract a grove of citrus from a grower. The contractor, who's called a "crew boss" in this area, employs the workers and receives a price per pound for the fruit, out of which he or she pays the workers. In this system, the contractor's wages are directly related to the pickers—higher if the contractor can hire the work

Cashmere, Washington, 1980.

done for less or if the pickers don't receive full payment for their work. This puts the contractor in a situation not unlike that of a grower in a smaller operation. In Florida, the growers are never seen; the pickers' only relationship to an employer is with the contractors.

When we worked in Florida, we met a crew bus every morning at six A.M. outside a twenty-four-hour cafe in downtown Lakeland. From there, we'd ride out to the orange and grapefruit groves in Polk City, Winterhaven, Auburndale, or Haines City.

The bus driver, Charlie, was also the contractor. Gregarious and shrewd, Charlie was about forty and had red hair that stuck out from under his baseball cap. He arranged the jobs, drove the tractor, did the bookkeeping, and paid the workers. On the way out to the fields, Charlie would stop the bus at a 7-Eleven store. About half of the crew were winos, and they would buy their day's supply of MD 20-20. Then there was a long drive

Contractor and his homemade jeep to transport ladders, Wenatchee Heights, Washington, 1974.

Seven A.M. wine and beer stop, Lakeland, Florida, 1974.

through the early morning mist to the citrus grove.

Even in ideal circumstances, work in the citrus is extremely difficult. Carrying large bags of fruit slung across one shoulder by a strap and bending over to pick up the heavy fallen fruit, a citrus picker places tremendous strain on his or her back. Although the winos were often teased about their drinking problems and slower work habits, they had to work incredibly hard just to pay their basic expenses for a hotel room, meals, and wine. They were often plagued with hangovers and exhaustion and were usually unable to work a whole day. Their productivity was about half that of other workers. Because of their dependence, they were very vulnerable to exploitation from unscrupulous contractors.

The return trip back to town at the end of the day was usually lively and entertaining, as pickers relaxed after the demanding work. Charlie stopped the bus at another convenience store and talked and joked with the pickers as he gave them their week's pay or a draw so they could buy wine. One man who rode on the crew bus had managed to overcome his addiction to wine by drinking a gallon of milk a day. We called him a "milko." He liked to sing bits of operas on the afternoon ride, creating a rather unusual atmosphere in the crew bus. Other people chatted about their workday and speculated about what the next day would bring. As he drove, Charlie interacted with the pickers, often promising them that the next day would bring better picking.

Charlie had a typical paternal relationship to the workers, more so than a contractor in the West usually has. He bailed them out of jail if they got into trouble, loaned them money if they ran short. But on the other hand, he took advantage of the winos' hazy memories. He would "give" them five dollars at the wine stop, and they were grateful for the money to spend on wine. But of course Charlie took the money out of their wages, and his accounting system was so casual there were many opportunities for mistakes made in his favor.

In the fields, too, Charlie kept total control over the wages. When he came by to pick up a bin, he jotted it down on a slip of paper next to the picker's name. He gave the pickers no record of their work, so if there was any discrepancy at the end of the day, only Charlie had a written record. Once when we disagreed with Charlie about the number of bins we'd picked, he acted as if we were personally insulting him. He looked to the other pickers on the bus for support, asking them loudly, "Haven't I always paid you right? Haven't I always been fair?" Embarrassed, we agreed to compromise and Charlie paid us for half of the bin we'd picked.

Even on a nonwino crew in Florida, contractors often seem to be at odds with pickers. Although the wino crews were

The "Rev" lightened his load with song. Winterhaven, Florida, 1974.

composed largely of single men, the nonwino crews included more couples, families, and some single women. They could not be exploited in the same way as winos, but the crew leaders took advantage of their time and labor in other ways.

Since workers are driven to the fields by the crew bus,

Earl Thomas, picker and contractor, Pasco, Washington, 1978.

they must remain there until the bus leaves, whether they are working or not. Sometimes workers are driven to the field before ladders and bins are set up for them, and they are forced to spend half a day waiting before they can begin to pick. Nearly every day pickers have to wait for the tractor drivers to bring them a new bin, and this can also take as long as half a day. Since pickers are paid by the piece-rate, contractors have little concern for their lost time. Even the pickers themselves consider the situation a lost cause and rarely complain.

On one job we had to wait with a large crew for the company to bring empty bins to a grapefruit grove. Since we couldn't pick, we just sat in the grove. Most of the crew, who'd come on the bus, would spend a large part of the day playing cards. At about one or two o'clock everybody was disgusted enough to go home, and the bus would leave. The truck with the bins did not arrive for three days! Such inefficiencies continue because no one protects the right of pickers. They are powerless, and the contractor doesn't take on the responsibility of representing them.

Also of little concern to the contractor is the amount of unproductive work the picker has to do in the fields. Workers carry terribly heavy twenty-five-foot wooden ladders long distances through the soft Florida sand. Just learning to carry and balance these ladders requires skill and practice. Though the contractor could make this task easier by carrying the ladders with their tractors, they very rarely do so. Even people with babies have to carry their ladders far across the fields, along with the baby, diapers, bottles, playpen, their food, and picking sacks. In general, contractors in Florida display little real concern for the pickers beyond an interest in how much they can profit from them.

In the West, a contractor usually plays a different role. The contractor, who is simply referred to as the person running the job, is often paid a flat rate by the grower, so his or her wages are not linked to the abilities of the pickers. Contractors often come from the ranks of fruit pickers, so their personal histories and characters are familiar.

In the West, contractors are almost always Hispanic or Anglo, and their crews generally share the same ethnic makeup. A combination of language barriers, cultural barriers, and prejudice (in both directions) causes this phenomenon. In recent years, there has been a proliferation of Hispanic contractors who effectively provide labor for growers and are highly valued for their bilingual capacities. As farmers switch to using Hispanic contractors, who are responsible for hiring the crew, Okies and other Anglos have been effectively excluded from available jobs. And even when Hispanics or Anglos find jobs on crews run by contractors of another ethnicity, they are frequently subjected to second-class treatment on the job. Everyday experiences in discrimination and competition for jobs have caused both groups to resent each other's presence in the fields, and contractors have played an important part in causing such resentment.

Working with Okie crews, our contractors were usually, but not always, men. Often their wives were responsible for the bookkeeping and payroll. It was very common to see older pickers begin to take on the role of contractor for one or more short harvests in the season, as their picking abilities waned with their age. Otis Brown, for example, worked as a contractor on the cherry job in California, then traveled north to Washington to work as a picker for the rest of the season. We had known him as a fellow picker for years before he took over as a contractor on one of our jobs after the former contractor suffered a heart attack.

Billy Baker switched from fruit picking to contracting after he hurt his back and could no longer pick; his knowledge of crops, pickers, and farmers served him well as a contractor, and he had a reputation among pickers as being exceptionally fair. He contracted jobs in the summer and managed a tavern in Idaho the rest of the year.

Earl Spicer, whom we worked for the first few years we picked cherries in Stockton, California, was part of a classic fruit-picking and contracting Okie family. The large extended-family network had settled around the orchard towns of Stockton and Porterville, California. In Stockton, many members of the Spicer clan lived in a seedy-looking trailer court called Cherry Lane. A little store in the front of the trailer court sold cherry buckets and harnesses as well as more standard commodities.

The younger members of the family traveled extensively on the fruit run and were reputed to be especially fast, if rough, pickers. We'd watch the Spicers with amazement as they ran up and down their ladders, their hands flying as they cleaned the branches of cherries, piled boxes of cherries beside their trees, and ran to the next set. We had a joke about "the Spicer break"—you unlatched your bucket with one hand, turned it upside down to sit on it for a moment, then swung it around, latched it up again, and resumed picking. The Spicers were a tough and hardy bunch of people who had made it in fruit picking by the sheer necessity of relentlessly hard work.

Earl and his wife, Ruby, had picked fruit on the West Coast for all of their long lives. With two other Spicer families, they'd recently moved to Emmett, Idaho, where they'd bought a mobile home. They used a small travel trailer for their annual migrations to California. In early spring they went to Porterville to visit their children. By May they were in Stockton, contracting jobs in the cherries, and then they went on to Washington, Montana, and Idaho to pick cherries and apples.

When we worked for Earl, a large percentage of the picking crew was made up of Spicers and their relatives. The few pickers who weren't related complained that the Spicers got all the best trees, but we couldn't see how this was possible: the number of family members exceeded the number of good trees. The old cherry trees towered to impossible heights. Rick picked the tops of the trees with a two-legged, tapered ladder called a spike, and I went around the bottom with a rickety wooden sixteen-foot ladder. After days of picking scrappy fruit, Earl finally took us to one tree that was loaded with cherries. "Boy, look at this one. It's really got the berries!" he exclaimed. He studied us intently with piercing blue eyes set in a lean and leathery face. "Some people say I give my relatives all the gravy,"

he said, "but that ain't true. See this tree I give you kids? It's the best tree in the orchard; it's just loaded with berries!" He stood for several minutes at the bottom of our ladders, admiring the tree.

Because most of the Okie contractors are well known as fruit pickers and may be part of large fruit-picking families, they are perceived as more trustworthy. They are, in fact, sympathetic to the problems of fruit pickers, but as employees of the grower their role can be ambiguous and confusing, to themselves as well as to the pickers.

"A lot of the people trust the contractor 'cause they know him as a picker, and they think, 'he's just like me,'" a friend confided to us. "But really he's working for the farmer and he gets hired to do things the way the farmer wants them. That man may be just like them when he's a picker, but when he's contracting, he don't have the pickers' interests at heart."

At best a contractor can manage the sporadic labor needs of the agricultural harvest while smoothing the frictions that can often occur between growers and pickers. At worst, he or she is caught in the middle of conflicting interests and is unable or unwilling to negotiate for the pickers.

The job of the contractor to act as an intermediary between pickers and growers has been used effectively to take the burden of responsibility for working conditions off the growers. If pickers are brought to an area for a job on the instructions of the grower, and then have to wait several weeks before they are able to work because of weather, market conditions, or the grower's miscalculation, they have no recourse. Because the grower has hired the contractor to be in charge of employment, the grower is absented from a share in the responsibility for the workers' problems.

Nevertheless pickers develop loyalties to certain contractors. People plan on coming back to a job because it is run well or fairly. "I liked the way Billy Baker ran that crew up in Wenatchee. It was like the old days, everything was straight, you took the sets in order. They'd even carry your ladders for you."

Often pickers will follow a contractor to the next job, putting faith in the contractor's ability to find good jobs and pay them fairly. Once when we finished a good job in Kennewick, we joined some of our co-workers in following the contractor to another job in nearby Benton City. Though the contractor did his

Milton-Freewater, Oregon, 1977.

Left: *Payday in the orchard at the contractor's car, Kennewick, Washington, 1982.*

job of organizing the work well, the orchard he took us to was scrappy and the pay didn't compensate for the poor picking. After several days of work, we regretted that we hadn't struck out on our own and found a better job. The cherry season is so short-lived that time spent working in a poor orchard is truly money lost.

We realized we had stuck with the contractor because of some misplaced sense of loyalty. As our friend Daniel said, "It seemed like we owed him something and we didn't owe him nothin'. That's one thing my father always did and I never did respect him for that—after he'd worked for a guy for awhile he'd go on working for him even if he was only making half of what he could be making somewheres else. I always said I never would do that. I wanna be free to quit a job if I don't like it."

Despite the ambivalent attitudes toward contractors and the problems associated with their position, there seems to be a real need for the job to exist, especially as farming operations become larger scale. A contractor may act as a mediator between two groups of people who are often unable to communicate their needs without serious misunderstandings and conflicts. And for many older pickers, contracting has been the only form of social security. When they're physically unable to make a living picking fruit anymore, they can often move into the contractor role with ease.

The problem with the contracting system is that it establishes an impersonal, once-removed relationship between grower and picker and allows the grower to treat the pickers as just another crop expense rather than as individuals with needs, skills, and human qualities. Through using contractors, growers may evade responsibility for the employment of pickers and help to perpetuate the idea that pickers are a sort of "untouchable" caste who can only be managed by other members of their group.

"There's always been contractors in agriculture," said one fruit picker philosophically. "That was one way the farmer had of gettin' his crop harvested without ever having to come in contact with what he considered to be a dirty element of society."

In Our Own Time
A Life outside Work

8. "You Meet All Kinds of People"
The Migrant Camp

Outside the city of Kennewick in southeastern Washington, we turn down a street that leads to the Columbia Center Mall and some other newer chain stores: K-Mart, Jafco, McDonald's. We continue past these structures, passing a new motel, an apartment complex, a bar and brand new streets of suburban one-story homes and ranchettes.

Most of this has been built in the last few years. Fifteen years ago, when we first came to this area, it was largely undeveloped. Irrigated orchards of cherries, prunes, and apples were interspersed with acres of dry desert land sprinkled with sagebrush. Now much of the open land is gone, as are many of the orchards. The groups of homes and apartment complexes that

Left: *A cherry camp, Stockton, California, 1975.*

have replaced them bear such names as "Cherry Acres" and "Orchard Homes."

Along one of the new little streets, we approach a windbreak row of tall poplar trees and turn down a familiar dirt road driveway. Pickers' trailers are parked in a long row along a fence that separates them from the backyards of the suburban houses. On the other side of the driveway, the cherry orchard begins, thirty acres of trees now surrounded on all sides by developments. Years ago, we'd return to this place three times during the summer to pick the cherries, prunes, and apples as they ripened in the adjacent orchards. But the prune and apple orchards were sold and torn up to make room for the more profitable dwellings.

The pickers' trailers, sandwiched between the new homes and the orchard, vary in size and style. They range from older, tiny thirteen-foot trailers to brand-new thirty-footers.

Pickers' trailers are parked between the orchard and a windbreak row of trees. Kennewick, Washington, 1978.

There are a couple of large painted buses, some campers, and one or two fifth-wheelers. At the side of the road as it curves into the orchard, there are a few tents and a couple of dilapidated trailers, parked without hook-ups.

After we pull our medium-sized, older trailer just outside the camp, we go to look for the farmer or the contractor. He, along with some of the other pickers, will help us get situated and set up camp.

A page from my journal typifies what it's like for a picker to get settled in a migrant camp:

16 May 1984
Arrived late last night (10 P.M.) and parked our car in the orchard just outside the camp. It was quiet but some people's lights were on, watching TV, so we figured there would be no picking in the morning. In the morning—five or six A.M.—we were awakened by crop dusters spraying the orchard next to us—a horrendous noise as they flew low over our trailer.

The men gather in their customary little group by the cherry trees next to the camp. Rick goes to talk to them. I say hello too. The women are invisible inside their trailers.

Otis (the contractor) shows us where to move our trailer. Floyd helps Rick back the trailer up. As we try to figure out electricity, water, etc., with Otis, another little group of men gathers. I begin digging the hole for the sewer. There are some teasing comments from the men, and one of them insists on taking the shovel from me to help until Rick can take over.

When we started picking fruit, we didn't have a trailer. We traveled in a Volkswagen van, camping out in the summer and staying in fruit-picker cabins in the fall when we picked pears and apples. But after we'd picked fruit for a couple of years, we began to see the advantages of owning our own home, no matter how small or simple. Our own trailer allowed us to make decisions about jobs without having to take available housing into consideration. Buying our first trailer was both a commitment to the migratory lifestyle and an opportunity to enjoy the domestic pleasures of a home without compromising our freedom to travel.

Although many of the Anglo fruit pickers now own their own trailers or campers, their first experience with the living conditions of orchard work was similar to that of agriculture's most recent immigrants today. In the 1930s and 1940s most of the Anglo pickers lived in tents.

"People lived in whatever they could," a picker recalled. "Lean-tos, tents, a cloth strung between two trees. A lot of people just lived in the back of a pickup. We did that quite often with our little children. I remember when we got our first trailer. Everybody came around and said, "Gee, he's rich! He's got a trailer; we've gotta live in these old tents."

Even today, in the summertime there are cherry orchards dotted with old tents and shelters made from cardboard and bin sides, where Hispanic pickers find temporary protection from the elements. Cabins provided for pickers in the fall have become more scarce. Years ago, the enforcement of regulations in housing caused many farmers to tear down their pickers' cabins. Now such enforcements are lax, but the effect of the regulations was a reduction in worker housing overall and little improvement in quality.

Even those pickers who own trailers are usually dependent on their employers to provide an adequate camp, preferably with water and electrical hook-ups. Pickers who own self-contained trailers have a greater measure of independence although they still need a place to park them. "What I like about a self-contained trailer is you always have hot water and you always have a bathroom, even when you're on the road or away from hook-ups for a long time," one picker told us. "Like one time

Independent life, Lake Alfred, Florida, 1977.

we camped along the road when we were working in Natchez. I sure was glad to have a self-contained trailer then."

Employers who don't allow pickers to camp in their orchard may effectively discriminate against the more established pickers. An entire area may have a tendency to make the Anglo pickers feel unwelcome. In *Wildcrafting: Harvesting the Wilds for a Living*, Jack McQuarrie comments on this aspect of migrant fruit picking. Almost all of the orchardists in the Yakima Valley in Washington do not allow pickers to camp on their property during harvest season. McQuarrie explains how pickers react to the prohibition:

This leaves pickers with two alternatives: the two local campgrounds which are, as a rule, not only jammed but mosquito ridden; and the area's motels, which raise their rates in honor of the occasion.

For these reasons, most experienced harvesters bypass the Yakima area altogether, leaving the work in that area to the "homeguards" and the increasing numbers of illegal Mexican aliens brought in each harvest season.[1]

Even in an area where many farmers allow pickers to camp in their fields, pickers without a job or with a job where they are not allowed to camp can find themselves with a serious problem. Parking their trucks or trailers at spots by the river is one solution but one the police don't generally tolerate. Local campgrounds in orchard areas are usually inadequate and too expensive for the needs of migrant pickers. They may also discriminate in favor of middle-class tourists. Few local trailer parks have spaces available for workers.

One summer we tried, with two other families, to find a place for our trailers while we looked for work. It was critical because one of the women we were traveling with, Darlene, was pregnant and due to have her baby any day. After finally finding a space at the county-run campground and paying extravagant tourist prices we could ill afford, we were told to leave two days later because the spaces were reserved for a group of motor homes.

We noticed that even after the motor homes had moved in there were still spaces in the campground—but all the fruit pickers had been told to leave. We talked to the sheriff, the public prosecutor, and finally the county commissioners, but all of them told us we had no recourse. We had become the criminals, forced to leave and camp at the only spot of land in the area where we knew we wouldn't be bothered. It was in the forest, twelve miles up a steep winding road from the town—a dangerous trip to take

at night when Daniel finally took Darlene to the hospital to have her baby.

Sometimes there is no good place for migrants to camp while they perform the labor that the community so depends on—even when they have provided their own mobile dwelling. But even in the worst of circumstances, migrants with trailers can take their homes with them when they leave.

Those migrants who have managed to buy new motor homes, campers, and trailers are in the minority, but they sym-

Home repairs, Wenatchee Heights, Washington, 1975.

Right: *Quincy, Washington, 1977.*

bolize the pickers' version of the American dream. Through them, pickers can transcend the stereotype that all migrants are dependent, destitute people, unable to better themselves.

A picker driving a new car or trailer blends in with the rest of the community so well that their occupation isn't obvious. To realize that a fruit picker is driving that new pickup and thirty-foot trailer, an observer would have to question the notion that pickers are trapped in the migrant life by their poverty. This contradiction can lead to funny incidents. "Be sure to lock your car—there are pickers in town," one migrant with a new car was told. "Aren't these cherry pickers awful?" another migrant was asked as an old homemade rig went by.

These comments are retold to other pickers with a mixture of humor and pain at the way they reflect discriminatory attitudes. "People see all these rough-looking people coming into town and they think all the fruit pickers are like that. They never see the rest of the pickers," Vicki commented.

Most of the people with the impressive new recreational vehicles started out in tents or homemade campers themselves. Saving their money during years of trading up older trailers, they've managed to buy a new trailer. To them, of course, it is not a "recreational vehicle" but a permanent or semipermanent home.

Darlene remembered well the hardships her family had gone through before they got enough money for a new trailer. "I can't understand some of these people who think they have to have a brand new trailer the first year they start out picking fruit," she commented. "We worked our way up. When we started we were sleeping in the back of a pickup—and we didn't have a camper neither! We lived in tents, and we used to have one of those little teardrop trailers. We had kids then too, and when it rained we all had to get inside that little old trailer and wait for it to stop raining so we could get out and eat. I'll never forget when we first got a new trailer. Daniel refused to buy it until we had every penny saved up to pay for it. He didn't want to buy it on payments. So we took all the money we'd saved up and went down and bought it."

Though most Anglo migrant camps consist mainly of trailers, often there are also tents, lean-tos, or homemade shel-

The camp washroom, Cashmere, Washington, 1976.

"Housing is nice when the weather turns nippy during the fall apple harvest but a roof over the head isn't something that most pickers worry about during the summer months," according to Jack McQuarrie in *Wildcrafting*. "Then it's enough just to wedge your tent or camper in among the others and make yourself right at home in the orchard of a farmer glad to have you. Two or three weeks in one of these instant communities can be a satisfying experience; you will meet fine people from all over the country."[2]

When we finish working in Kennewick, we hitch our trailer to our car and move it to an orchard outside of Pasco, a town ten miles from Kennewick. From Pasco we drive another half hour out to a countryside dominated by the presence of the Hanford Nuclear Plant. On either side of the road there are fields of asparagus, wheat, and alfalfa, broken by an occasional orchard. Spray planes fly low over the crops, dusting them with herbicides; the cloud of spray drifts lazily across the border of the field. A cherry orchard is tucked away here behind a field of asparagus.

Some distance from the grower's house, there is a clearing for the trailers and campers. One tree provides shade for the lucky people who got here early enough to park under it. We've arrived too late for shade, so we take our place behind another trailer and begin digging a hole for our sewer hose. The trailers and cars form a loose circle, parked closely together. The extension cords and hoses run over the ground to a few outlets and spigots.

Before work begins, the camp is active—full of the sounds of kids playing, people conversing, trucks coming and going. A section from my journal describes the sounds of the camp at night:

Luxury in the cherry camp, Kennewick, Washington, 1976.

ters of plastic and apple bins, especially during cherry picking when the warm weather is kinder to those with temporary homes. For the hobos who ride the rails, camping is often as simple as a bedroll on the ground near the tracks. "I can't understand why people want to go camp out," said one hobo. "I've been camping out all my life." Another hobo told us he'd spent the night sleeping in the dirt down by the river. "Can't tell myself from the ground," he said. In colder weather, hobos waiting for work must find shelter in the Salvation Army or missions if they don't mind being preached at—or join the other homeless people until they find work and a place to stay.

Flathead Lake, Montana, 1978.

27 May 1982

Tonight the camp is active and noisy till ten o'clock; a Saturday night with no work tomorrow. A radio plays in someone's trailer, a baby cries, and from time to time a woman yells, "Quiet!" I wonder whether she yells at the baby or the person with the radio. The baby probably.

The dogs bark and someone yells, "Cocoa! Shut up!" After ten the camp is quiet but at eleven a truck comes in and I hear voices again. Some more trailers light up and radios and TVs come on. It's the trailer next to us. I can hear the water running and the opening and closing of cabinets. The artificial voice of a TV announcer.

The paper-thin walls of the trailers let every sound travel through; privacy in a migrant camp is close to impossible. But once work begins, people obey certain unwritten rules: after nine or ten o'clock there must be quiet. Cherry picking begins espe-

cially early in the morning and pickers need adequate sleep to have the energy for the long hours of intense work.

Once picking has started, the camp is deserted from the early morning to the middle of the afternoon. Sometimes a pregnant woman stays at home a little later in the morning caring for her toddler, or someone comes in from the field for more water or their lunch or a forgotten ticket book—but other than that, it's quiet.

After two o'clock, people begin to drift back to camp, their talking and the clanging of cherry buckets breaking the silence. Trucks roar in and out of camp as people return from work and leave again to buy groceries; the dogs sleeping in the shade under the trailers wake and bark. There is an occasional sound of pop tops opening as people consume cold sodas or beers after work. Each day seems to have its own pattern. Some days everyone drives off or disappears into their trailers to shower and rest after work, and the camp is quiet again until the late afternoon. On other days a more social mood prevails, and people pull up their folding lawn chairs to sit under the trees or in the shade of a trailer, talking and visiting until supper time. Kids run through the dust and splash around in the irrigation ditch near the orchard. A couple of older kids ride their three-wheeler motorbikes through the orchards, punctuating the conversations with an irritating buzz.

Supper time is usually early—about five o'clock. The women go back in the trailers first, to cook. They call out to their daughters: "Jenny, help me peel these taters!" Later they call to the menfolk: "Come git yer supper!" The men reluctantly push back their chairs.

"Well, I'd better be goin'. We're havin' meat for dinner tonight."

"Meat! Hey, you must've made a lot of money today! Ain't you invitin' us over? That reminds me of the story of that guy in Oklahoma—he didn't have no money and he took his gal to the carnival and she says, 'Gee, that popcorn sure smells good.' And he says, 'Why don't you get a little closer—you can smell it better!'"

"Well, ya'all just move a little closer to the trailer so's you can smell that hamburger meat!"

"I best be goin' to my own trailer. Martha's fixin' steak for supper—some of that baloney steak!"

The men continue joking as they break off from the group, heading for their nearby trailers.

A tent and the back of a pickup make a temporary home. Big Arm, Montana, 1977.

After supper people again move out of their trailers, now too warm from the afternoon cooking, into the cooler air of the evening. The summer sky is still bright, long from sunset. The folding chairs are rearranged. Sometimes everyone will sit together in a wide circle; other times they divide into male and female groups. The men walk out into the orchard together or lean against the side of a pickup, sipping beer. In some camps, the men gather in a circle in the dust to gamble.

The women stay close to the trailers, watching the babies and toddlers, gossiping and talking "women talk."

One evening in a camp in Cove, Oregon, I joined a group of women near Joyce's trailer. Joyce was in her early twenties and lived with her husband and two small children in a tiny, overcrowded trailer. She had been picking fruit since she was twelve; her husband had picked all his life. They were fast pickers even though they watched two small children as they picked.

Joyce filled a big plastic container with water from the spigot and carried it back to the trailer for the childrens' bath. The other women sat on folding chairs or overturned cherry buckets by the trailer door, talking of work and children. I'd watched Joyce in the orchard, running up and down the ladder, caring for her children in between picking. I asked her if it wasn't hard to work with little children. "No," she said, laughing, "it gives me someone to holler at!" "No, really," she continued, "I can't stand to hear a baby cryin', so I always go down and hold her awhile, but besides that, they don't really take up that much of my time."

Mattie, whose youngest was eight at the time, agreed, "I always did like having a baby in the field. You could go down for a few minutes and take a break and it would perk you right up."

Pat, a pale and rawboned woman, sat in a folding chair near the trailer. She was eight months pregnant. "I wished I'd of planned this baby for winter. Then you can pick all the cherries, pears, and apples; have the baby; and go back to work the next spring. But this way I'm gonna lose a week of work right in the middle of the cherries. And I haven't been able to pick much bein' pregnant. Alls I can do is put the bucket on the ground and help pick the bottoms."

"Where do you think you'll be when you have this baby?" I ask.

"Wenatchee, I reckon," said Pat. "I'll just go in to that hospital there when it's time. I never did see no doctors about it—just too much movin' around, and those doctors don't want nothin' to do with you unless you start out with them. When you're a fruit picker, they don't even want you in them hospitals very long. You just have the baby at night, and you're out the next morning. But they charge you the same as if you'd been going to the doctor all nine months."

Darlene nodded, "Oh, they can be terrible at the hospital. They make you feel so dirty anyway, bein' as you're a migrant, and if you ain't had a shower in three or four days, you really do feel bad. I remember when I had Lavonna, down in The Dalles; they took her and separated her from all the other babies. She was off in a room all by herself! I guess they thought she was contaminated or something. They told me they was doing it to see if there was anything wrong with her, because they didn't have a record on me or anything."

The talk about pregnancy and childbirth drifts on. The women ask me when I'm going to have a child. They find it very

Right: *"I'm gonna lose a week of work in the middle of the cherries." Kennewick, Washington, 1977.*

Far Right: *Games, talk, and laundry before breaking up camp, Stockton, California, 1976.*

odd that I don't have a few at my age—twenty-eight at the time—and probably think I have a fertility problem. Most of them are married and have at least one child by eighteen. That's what a woman is supposed to do in this culture. They discuss a mutual friend: "She needs to have another baby to settle her down."

The conversation is interrupted constantly by children. "Mama, I need to go potty!" "Jackie hit me with a stick!" The babies need to be fed and changed; the toddlers need to be restrained from putting everything in their mouths, playing with outlets, and countless other hazards. The older children appear occasionally, demanding "cold sody pops" to quench their thirst.

As dusk settles over the camp, the women break apart, collect their children, and go home to put them to bed. A few people linger outside, savoring the last few moments of leisure in the day, but soon they go in their trailers too. By 9:30 the camp is quiet and darkness descends.

Not all camps are as quiet or orderly as the camps we stayed at in Kennewick and Cove. Each camp has its own character, determined by the space provided by the grower, the pickers who work there, and the contractor, who often determines both who is hired and the conditions of the camp.

Pickers may decide against a job if the camp is too rough. "There don't seem to be near as much fighting in these camps or courts anymore," said one older picker. "I guess they just keep some of these wilder guys out of them. But some of them camps, I wouldn't go into. If there's drinkin' and fightin' and it's noisy, I just won't go into 'em."

Ruby, an older woman with bright blue eyes and a pleasantly crinkled face, ran a large crew in Stockton, California, with her husband. She also took care of the orchard camp where they lived.

Oh, most of the people we have are real fine people—family people, you know, but sometimes we have some real dingoes. We try to keep a camp real clean, but last year we didn't keep a real good watch on it, and oh, we had a mess! We had a stripper in here—I don't know where that old gal came from. We hired this one guy and then he brought his friend who we didn't even hire. And one morning Earl had to go wake him up at nine o'clock—he still hadn't come out to work yet! And he sees that gal running around the camp with nothing on but a little shirt, and the old man chasing after her! Well, we told them to go on down the

Few camps provide shower facilities. Lodi, California, 1985.

Right: *The camp laundromat, Cove, Oregon, 1978.*

road. Yes, you see all kinds of things doing this work. You meet all kinds of people. Ninety-nine percent of them are fine, upstanding people. But let me tell you, you do get your share of beanbags!

Many camps are occupied predominantly by large family clans. The different characteristics of the clans give the camp its character. This can vary widely: in some camps drinking and gambling in the evening provide entertainment, while in others fundamentalist church meetings are a focus of evening activity. Neither extreme is typical, but both exist.

These family-dominated pickers' camps are particularly insulated from the rest of society. The extended families depend on the nearest town for supplies but little else. The community of the camp provides family life, work, relaxation, and entertainment. Interrelated groups of families and old friends tend to stay together as much as possible. They may drift apart on one job but come back together on the next one, like woven threads.

Even when members of an extended family are living at different camps, they usually work in the same area and will often visit each other in the evenings. The sense of family is so strong that when friends came to visit us at the migrant camp, people invariably referred to them as our sisters or brothers, even though we had explained that they weren't related.

Since fruit pickers are likely to marry other pickers, many of the large families are interrelated. Sometimes the relationships in one camp are too complex to remember. As big Okie fruit-picker families grow more scarce, the remaining families become more tied together through marriages.

Families develop reputations in both lifestyles and in their work. One extended family will be known for "clean" (careful, quality) picking and a family-oriented lifestyle, while another is known for their "rough" (fast, sloppy) picking, their drinking, gambling, and careless ways.

Okies generally have very large families and the Okie-dominated camps are usually full of children. Even those people who engage in drinking and gambling are still strongly connected to their families because the life of the camp is so inclusive. These activities don't usually take place in a bar or other place separate from home; all activities become part of the public life of the camp.

When we went to visit friends at an orchard camp in Milton-Freewater, Oregon, the men in camp were squatting in the dirt, throwing dice into the center of their circle. On the edges of the circle, some children stood and watched with interest,

Fight in the camp, Pasco, Washington, 1979.

while others rode by on their bikes. The contractor, who was related to many of the pickers, was in the circle too. He drank beer and added up the paychecks, fueling the gambling with more funds. At the same time he bounced a baby on his knee, distracting the little boy from crying about a coffee burn. Women flitted in and out of each others' trailers, as if their homes were commonly owned. Sometimes the women came out to the men's circle to watch, comment, deposit or retrieve a child, or secure their grocery money before it was lost.

As interrelated families and co-workers share the same limited living space, with little privacy or outside distraction, tensions and conflicts naturally develop. Often they can be relieved by the mobile nature of fruit picking. Deciding to switch jobs and work away from another family for awhile is a common way of avoiding further conflict.

Sometimes, however, disputes erupt into fights in the camp. Often these are between family members. Once, in a camp in Stockton, I heard gunshots in the night. Afraid to go out and see what was happening, I locked our trailer door. The next day I learned that a man had been having an argument with his son-in-law and had shot the gun into the air for effect. Another time, when we worked with a rough crew in Stockton, a mother accused her daughter of bird-dogging her tree, and they had a physical fight in the orchard, pulling each others' hair.

One time when we were sitting around a camp in the evening talking with our co-workers, we heard loud, angry voices. A woman was having an argument with her son-in-law. The pickers moved closer to see what was going on. Another man who'd been drinking got in the argument too. The people watching said there'd been gambling, which had caused the disagreement. As everyone in camp stood at a distance and watched, the two men wrestled with each other. No one was hurt, but the wrestling was followed by more insults and verbal abuse. Watching the interaction, the pickers seemed both disturbed and amused by it. As the fight broke up, people moved back towards their trailers, talking quietly, "Boy, they really got into it! I wouldn't be surprised if his trailer wasn't here in the mornin'."

Although these family fights occured occasionally, it was rare to see them erupt into physical abuse. The three incidents described above were the only ones we witnessed in more than ten seasons of living in migrant camps, although we heard of many more occuring in other camps. A more common response to personal conflict or to work-related dissatisfaction was to leave—often pickers would pull their trailers out during the night as an expression of their anger. We were frequently surprised by the empty places in the morning, and after asking around we often found that a disagreement with a relative, contractor, farmer, or co-worker had provoked the departure.

Pickers are less likely to leave to protest their living conditions. Because the jobs are so temporary, they'll often tolerate unsatisfactory conditions. Even when they live in their own modern trailers, they may lack conveniences (water, sewer, electricity) if a grower does not supply them. Those without trailers may live in worse conditions in cabins or tents, with run-down outhouses and irrigation canals as their only facilities.

Still, pickers value being able to camp without paying, often right next to where they work. They save time, money, and energy and they can spend leisure time with their family and friends. Since they are seldom at a single camp for more than two weeks, they can tolerate poor conditions. Of course, migrants often live with unsatisfactory conditions for much longer periods of time, because moving to another job doesn't always improve their situation.

Because growers are not required to provide pickers with a place to live at all, and because regulations concerning living conditions have had the effect of eliminating many pickers' camps altogether, migrants don't express a particular sense of blame for the poor conditions of some camps, even though such conditions reinforce community attitudes that migrants are unclean. Migrants are apt to feel grateful to those growers who do spend their time and money to make the pickers' camps liveable for the families who work there, and they evaluate what a camp is like as well as what the crop looks like in making job choices. But their first priority is their work, and even with the best living conditions, a picker may leave if he hears of better picking elsewhere. A fruit-picker joke that we heard in camp one afternoon illustrates that point:

A guy went to heaven and the camp was full. So he said, "Well, that's alright—there'll be room in the morning." Then he went around to everybody and told them, "They're gonna start picking cherries in hell in the morning and those cherries are really big!" Well, the next morning the camp in heaven was empty and God asked, "Where'd everybody go?" The guy said, "They all went to hell 'cause they heard the cherries was better over there!"

The life of the camp is so intertwined with the work itself that one blends into the other with little distinction. Conversations in the migrant camp focus on work—pickers are never far away from their work physically or emotionally. These casual gatherings after work are the core of much that happens in pickers' lives. This is where rumors are begun or spread about other crops and jobs, causing pickers to avoid or seek out a certain job or area. Pickers pass on information about future jobs gleaned from phone calls to growers and word of mouth from other pickers. The gatherings are also where job dissatisfaction

Right: *Picker's cabin, Okanogan, Washington, 1978.*

is expressed and, more rarely, where organized expressions of dissatisfaction are initiated.

The migrant camp itself is at the heart of the migrant life. It is the scene of family and community life, work and play— the place where private and public life, work and leisure intermingle. As temporary as the camp may be, for a migrant, it is home.

9. "Ya'all Wanna Come in the House for Some Iced Tea?" *Leisure Time*

On a June morning, in the height of the picking season, I awoke to the sound of raindrops drumming on the metal roof of our trailer. With relief, I shut off the alarm and turned over to go back to sleep. Rain meant there would be no work that day, a rare day of leisure on the cherry run. Cherries can't be picked while they're wet or they will rot and mold in the boxes. Growers and pickers worry about rain for another reason too: when the cherries are ripe a heavy rain, especially if it's followed by sunshine, can cause the cherries to swell up and split, making them worthless for the fresh-fruit market. Potential damage by rain is one of the reasons cherries are known as a high-risk crop.

Left: *Kennewick, Washington, 1975.*

On this morning, however, I felt more grateful than worried about the rain. We'd already worked seven days in a row, and I needed a day off. Like the other pickers, our day off consisted of enjoying a hot breakfast at home or at a cafe and doing the chores we had put off the last week, like laundry and shopping. Sometimes we spent part of the day driving around to rummage sales or store sales, satisfying material desires on a low-income budget. And our day off always left time for "visiting," that all-important social activity for pickers.

Leisure time occurs on these rainy days, and on days when fruit pickers wait for work to begin, either between jobs, or when they are laid off because the fruit isn't ripe enough. There is also some leisure time in the hours after work.

On a rainy day, pickers visit their friends and relatives in each others' trailers, but in better weather people sit outside on folding chairs, talking for hours. This is the time when people reinforce their connection to the community of migrants, often visiting people who are working in other orchards.

The rain had stopped by ten o'clock that morning, but the orchard was still wet. Water dripped off the leaves of the trees and settled around the base of the cherry stems. There would be no picking that day. The grower had arranged for helicopters to come and fly over the field. This is an expensive operation but the wind stirred up by the rotor dries the cherries and minimizes the risk of damage, salvaging the rest of the crop.

After we'd been told by the contractor that we wouldn't go back to work that day, we finished our backlog of chores and then drove to another migrant camp to visit some friends. A mixed group of about eight people sat outside talking; they found folding chairs for us so we could join them. As usual there was much joking and casual conversation, interspersed with more serious talk.

"I hope we can get back to work in the morning and work straight through," one picker said. "I need to pull this rig up to Bridgeport right quick—Al says they're starting up there the twenty-third."

"That'd be early for up there," someone else commented. "I never have started up there much before the first."

"Well, I'm glad to have the day off," said an older man. "Those cherries have been coming off hard, and I'm about wore out on this job. You know the saying: 'I like work so much, I could lie right down beside of it and go to sleep.'"

Pasco, Washington, 1978.

Right: *Small talk and family life are principal forms of entertainment. Big Arm, Montana, 1977.*

"Maybe if he'd raise the price up another quarter, we'd feel more like pickin' his crop," a heavyset woman suggested.

"Yeah, they'll pay another quarter a box up north, and for better cherries too," a lean, middle-aged man said. "Say, did you ever hear the one about how the guy come out in the orchard and asked the farmer, 'How much are you payin?' The farmer said, 'I'll pay you what you're worth' and the picker says, 'Hell, I won't work that cheap!'"

We laughed at the joke with everyone else as we savored the time to sit and talk, enjoying the easy rapport with other pickers. The moment was interrupted by a woman who came up to her husband to ask him for grocery money.

"What'd you do with that five spot I gave ya last week?"

"You know the saying, 'I like work so much, I could lie right down beside of it and go to sleep.'" Pasco, Washington, 1978.

Right: *Storytelling is a practiced art. Flathead Lake, Montana, 1978.*

he teased her. He held out the money to her and then pulled it away as she reached for it. At last he gave it to her. Scenes like this reminded me of how the women, who work as equals with the men, are degraded by jokes and teasing. Okies tend to view women traditionally, as second-class citizens, and their domestic work is taken for granted. In the field, men refer to the women as their "helpers." "Where's your helper this mornin'?" "Oh, she's gettin' the baby." "She run out on you again, did she?"

The incident had the effect of dividing the conversation. Now the women talked among themselves about clothes, wash, and children. We talked about the rummage sales we'd been to that day. "I found some real good ones today," Darla said. "I got a big old bag of clothes for fifty cents. And some baby clothes for a dime apiece. Some people say, 'I wouldn't put no used clothes on my brand new baby.' Well, shoot! If it wasn't for these used clothes, I wouldn't have nothin' at all."

I listened absently to the women talk, while the men on the other side of me talked about fishing. "That Pete always was a good one for a fish story," said a robust man. "If somebody'd ask him something in the mornin' he'd say, 'Don't make me start lyin' this early in the mornin'.' He'd say that ever' mornin'. 'Long about noon, he'd really start tellin' some stories."

"When I was a kid, they used to really have some fish back there on the Sacramento River," began Clyde, an older man. He leaned forward in his chair, propping an elbow on one crossed knee. "There was a guy out there who could really catch those fish. He'd come back to the camp every night and tell us stories about some big fish he'd caught that day. Once he told us he'd been using a clothesline for his fishing line and a big old fish come along and bit that rope clean in two. So the next day he went out and got him a big old hoist chain and he took one of those leaf springs out of the back of a Model A and he just bent that like a hook. He hooked the chain on the back of that Model A

Flathead Lake, Montana, 1978.

and tried to pull that fish in. Well, that fish got aholt of that chain and no one's seen that Model A since!"

The men burst into laughter, and some of the women who overheard the story chuckled too.

"We-ell . . . " drawled one of the men, addressing the other men. "Let's go and have a look at them cherries and see if the rain's hurt 'em any." The men got up and walked toward the orchard.

Martha rose from her chair too. A tall, lean middle-aged woman, she had a striking but rugged beauty. "Ya'all wanna come in the house for some iced tea?"

A big TV and a twelve-foot-wide trailer, Bridgeport, Washington, 1977.

The two other women and I followed her to her trailer. She poured sweetened instant iced tea from a pitcher into plastic glasses. Then she flipped on a small black and white TV set. "All My Children" came on, without the sound. "I'd like to catch up on what's goin' on here," she said. "These days it rains is the only time I get a chanct."

"I know it," Bobbie agreed. She was shorter than Martha, with pale hair pulled into a pony tail, and a sunburned, freckled face. "Don never wants to let me go to the house to fix lunch fer I might stay and watch the soap oprys," she laughs.

The women's talk about soap opera characters drifted so casually into talk about people they knew that I often couldn't tell one from the other. Darla, her pretty face hardened from fifteen years of raising children, settled herself on the couch with her glass of iced tea in hand. As a commercial came on the TV, she started to talk.

"You know Paula? I saw her the other day where they're pickin' out on Hammer Lane. She was tellin' me how she left Frank last month and took one of the cars and over half the money. She got all the way up to Modesto and she'd done spent all the money so she called up Frank and told him to come on up and get her. So he said, 'Why don't you just come on home? It's gonna take the rest of our money and gas for two cars if I go get you.' But she said, 'No—if you love me, you'd better come get me!' Then she hung up. Well he went down there and got her alright!" Darla sighed. "I know Jim wouldn't let me get away with that!"

"Well, Evelyn's another one for running away," said Bobbie. "She packed up her clothes and stuff so many times and then she'd have to come back and put everything away again. Finally, she just told Jack he could keep all her stuff the next time she left."

Martha laughed. "The way I heard it, she just kept her clothes packed all the time, ready to go. Reminds me of Bill Clayton's wife. Everytime she'd run away, he'd burn up all her clothes. But she didn't mind it, 'cuz when she got back, he'd buy her a whole new wardrobe!"

The women shake their heads. "The worst of the lot is Geraldine!" exclaimed Bobbie. "That woman is always badgering H. B. for more stuff. When they had a camper to live in, that was just not good enough for her—she never even unpacked anything; she just lived out of suitcases and boxes for months. So at last he bought her a new trailer and got it paid for. But the last few months she's been complaining about that—now she wants a brand new fifth-wheel!"

"If you ask me, that woman is spoilt," Darla said. "She

Right: *Taking the six-raw-egg dare, Pasco, Washington, 1978.*

don't really have any cause to complain, now that H. B.'s cut down on his drinkin', and besides that, he gives her all the money she wants."

"Well, speakin' of people leavin', the women ain't the only ones to leave," Martha grinned. "Yeah, Tommy tried to leave me three times in one night! He left and then he came right back and said he forgot his coat. So I gave him his coat and he left. Then about an hour later he was back wanting his gun. Well, he got his gun and took off again. Another hour and a half he was back again—he wanted his clothes that time. Then he went away again, but when I got up the next mornin', there he was, asleep in the truck!"

The commercial over, Martha turned up the volume on the TV. The theme music from "All My Children" came on, and the women's eyes turned toward the set. The camera focused on a beautiful, wealthy woman with a look of sinister seductiveness. "Oh, I hate her," Bobbie murmured. "She's done everything she can to break up that poor girl's home, and you know she don't really give a hoot about Cliff."

The conversation turned to a running commentary on the soap opera as television took precedence over personal stories.

Bill Taylor, Wenatchee, Washington, 1981.

Although TV shows sometimes become the subject of conversations, pickers usually prefer socializing to watching television. On long days off, those people with newer, air-conditioned trailers may stay inside to watch TV, but usually even they find it difficult to resist the jovial familiarity of a group of pickers gathered under a shade tree.

On occasion, pickers will go out for entertainment on a day off or after work. There is more going out after a job has begun; before that it's difficult to afford the luxury. Pickers usually have simple tastes: going out to eat pizza, fried chicken, or hamburgers is an occasion, and often pickers like to take their children or go out as a group with other families. More rarely, a couple will dress up and go out to eat at a steak house. Pickers seldom go out dancing or to movies—these activities are too late for people who habitually rise at dawn—but they do take advantage of rural entertainment such as county fairs, carnivals, and swap meets.

Although going out is refreshing, it takes second place to the important social and leisure life of the migrant camp. Migrants feel strongly their isolation from the rest of the community and rarely try to integrate themselves in it. They are most relaxed among themselves.

Singing, guitar playing, and campfires used to be a part of the social life of migrants. They are not entirely gone, but radios, tapes, and television have largely replaced homemade entertainment. More modern housing curtails the outdoor social gatherings, as people choose more individual comfort. Some pickers who remember the old days are nostalgic for those times.

"I don't know where all the people went that used to work in the fields, but I miss 'em," Daniel told us sadly one evening. "And things like singin' on the loudspeakers to the pickers, gamblin', shootin' dice around the end of the pea rows and cotton rows. I miss campin' out in the tamarack trees and all the unusual people that you used to meet—like the storytellers and the old men with their boxes of tricks and musicians and whittlers. Anymore, it's just a businesslike group of people that the growers are after. The real model fruit pickers are all that's really got a chance anymore."

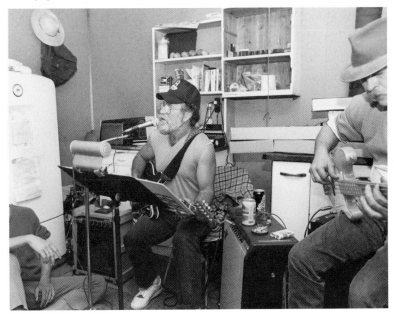

After harvest jam, Cashmere, Washington, 1989.

As Daniel perceived, much of the richness of social life and the folk arts has been lost as people become more economically comfortable in a standardized culture, more isolated yet less resourceful. But pickers tend to reflect the changes in the larger society more slowly. Although the singing and the campfires have all but disappeared, on a summer evening in a migrant camp the art of conversation with fellow pickers is still very much alive.

10. "We've Always Lived the Kind of Life That Was Pleasing to God"
Religion and Morality

"We follow the word of God, instead of just doing what we want," Gerald was explaining to us one day during a coffee break in the orchard. A young man with sandy-colored hair and a serious demeanor, he lay on the hard ground, propping himself up on his elbow. "It's hard sometimes going against the desires of the flesh," he went on, "but we have to think that we have all of eternity ahead of us."

Gerald and his wife, Maxine, were members of a fundamentalist religion, a branch of The True Followers of Christ. Maxine's father, Slim O'Neill, was a preacher, and together with extended family members, friends, and new converts—all of

Left: *Church service in a cherry orchard, Stockton, California, 1981.*

them fruit pickers—they attended church meetings in the orchards. "We don't believe the church is in a building. The church is the body of Christ," Maxine said, as she gave her baby a drink of milk from a mason jar. She was tall and thin, her lovely face framed by long dark hair that she covered for work with a bandana. She wore an old dress with work pants underneath and dressed her daughters similarly. Their religion dictated that women should not wear men's clothing, but pants could be worn under a skirt as a concession to the realities of fruit picking.

Maxine elaborated on some of the beliefs of their religion as we listened with fascination. "We just believe in the Bible exactly as it's wrote down," she continued. "We believe in healing with laying on of hands; we don't believe in hospitals or doctors. When the kids are sick, we just pray for them. And we believe in touching serpents. For the Bible says, 'You shall touch serpents.' We don't bring snakes to the meeting, but if we ever see a snake, we'll pick it up. In Florida, I picked up a lot of them."

Because we were genuinely interested in their religion (although we made it clear that we weren't interested in converting), Gerald and Maxine invited us to go with them to a meeting. It took place in an orchard, twice a week, in whatever area the migrants were working. On a Wednesday evening, after work and a light supper, we joined them in their car and drove for about twenty minutes along the rural backroads until we reached the orchard where the meeting was being held.

We pulled into the pickers' camp, where trailers, tents, and campers were crowded together between the cherry trees. As we got out of the car, I was struck by the number of children in the camp. They filled the air with their noise and energy, as they ran and bicycled up and down the orchard road, teasing and challenging each other. We walked past them into the orchard camp. Between two trailers there was a circle of folding chairs, cherry buckets, and boxes where people had already gathered

for the meeting. There were about twenty-five or thirty people, many of whom I recognized as Maxine's relatives. Her father, Slim, walked into the center of the circle and began preaching about the sins of "lusts of the flesh."

How can one be reborn? he asked rhetorically. "There is nothing here for the flesh, no fulfillment for the lust of the flesh. The flesh has to die for the soul to live."

His hand on the closed Bible, and his eyes half shut, Slim emanated religious intensity as he recited long passages of the Scriptures. The gathering of men and women and a few older children listened intently to this powerful speaker. A tall man with a ruddy complexion, Slim had been preaching religion since he was a teenager. He was a logger in Idaho until his wife died, leaving him with a dozen children. Then he took off with the children in a homemade camper and started traveling around

Migrant churches don't need a roof. Stockton, California, 1981.

the country picking fruit. Now married to a Mexican woman with whom he's had a couple more children, he continues to pick fruit, preaching at these meetings at every stop along the fruit run.

After Slim's sermon, people took out their songbooks and sang together. Then they bowed their heads as a different preacher led them in silent prayer. After prayer, several people got up to talk spontaneously to the group, telling how they had turned from a life of sin. Then another preacher got up to address the group.

Although the preachers were all male, a majority of the people at the meeting were female. I recognized Slim's daughters interspersed around the group. Some of their faces were bony and narrow, others wide and full, but all shared the same dark hair and strong, fine features. Many of them had babies or toddlers on their laps or clinging to their skirts. There were other women here that I recognized as well. Many of them had husbands who would come to the meetings for a while, then backslide into their sacrilegious habits, drinking and gambling.

As the meeting continued, I became aware of the other activities in the surrounding camp. Down the row from where we sat, trailer doors opened and shut, people talked, and children ran and shouted on the road, carrying a bird that had fallen from the nest. Half of the camp remained disconnected from the religious fervor of the meeting.

For over an hour the meeting went on, following the pattern of preaching interspersed with singing and praying. A reading from the New Testament was followed by a song in Spanish, a concession to the four or five Mexicans who attended the meeting. The meeting closed after a short personal testimony by someone who had recently joined the religion.

After the meeting, Slim asked everyone to stay for coffee. Several of the women went into the trailer next to us to make the coffee. We were introduced to the other two preachers and other church members. The church members kissed each other in greeting, a practice that Maxine later explained as deriving from a Biblical reference. It seemed especially noticeable because fruit pickers rarely hug or touch in greeting—Okies are generally reserved about physical contact.

As everyone socialized and drank their coffee, one of the preachers talked animatedly to us. He was very interested in how and why we'd come to a meeting. We asked him if there were many of these "church" meetings among migrants.

"No," he shook his head. "You look around most of these camps in the evening, the guys are throwing dice! Most of those people think we're crazy for what we believe in. But you know, we believe the Lord will take care of us. Before we found God, the doctors said we would never have children and now my wife has two babies!"

"Yeah," agrees Maxine. "We don't believe in goin' to the hospitals—that's why we have 'em at home. You know, I had one baby and it died. They said I had RH negative blood and couldn't have no more babies—they could die or be retarded. But after I got baptized, I had two—and now I got two spoiled brats!" she grinned.

Since the religion does not believe in birth control, the children outnumber the adults in the group. One time when we went to visit Maxine on a rainy day in late autumn, her trailer was crowded with her three sisters and at least a dozen children, packed like sardines inside the tiny living area of the trailer. Maxine sounded a little despairing. "I wish the Lord would stop sending us so many children!"

The fundamentalist religion that Maxine and Gerald belong to has few members among migrants, but many other Okie migrants share a similar religious background. When we stayed with fruit-picker friends in Texas, we visited their Pentecostal church, where the people (again, mostly women) talked in tongues and sometimes ran down the aisles, motivated by the Holy Spirit. Songs were sung to the accompaniment of accordion, guitar, and piano. From our friends, we were already familiar with some of the prohibitions of the church. Basically, all entertainment outside the church was banned; members could not watch movies, television, or even rodeo; they could not listen to the radio or go to dances, or consume any alcohol. Women were not allowed to wear men's trousers, and the women who worked in the fields wore dresses over their blue jeans. Jewelry, including watches, and makeup were also forbidden.

The social pressures on people in a close-knit community to belong to such a church can be overwhelming. But being migratory, fruit pickers often drift in and out of religious associations and behavior. Even those who try to keep the faith far from home often stretch restrictions to suit their lifestyle. For example, we've rarely met any fruit picker who refused to work on Sunday for religious reasons. In agricultural work, you are expected to work every day of the harvest that weather permits (at least with crops that are harvested in less than two or three weeks).

Fruit pickers traveling from town to town rarely find churches like the ones they are used to. Darlene told us, "There's Pentecostal churches out here, but they ain't like the ones back home." In the past, traveling preachers and missionaries among pickers provided a religious community for migrants. "Churches used to send out missionaries to migrant workers," Paul recollected. "Those missionaries would follow around wherever the migrant workers went and hold services in the camp. They were livin' in the same conditions as the migrant workers themselves were. I thought it was really a good thing to have people there to bring the word of God to people that were working, who maybe didn't have acceptable clothes to go to a big church service in

town—they could have church right among themselves in the camp. I thought this was a pretty good thing to do, although it don't never seem to be done anymore."

One missionary couple that was well remembered by many migrants were Brother and Sister Johnson. They traveled among fruit pickers, holding church meetings in the orchard and distributing charity where it was needed. "You know, they used to get a lot of money that people donated to them," Walter remembered. "There was one lady in Hollywood that used to send them five hundred dollars a month. But it was money for the poor people, and that old man never did spend any of it on himself."

Darlene also recalled the couple fondly. "I remember they used to have that old car all loaded up with clothes that people give them in Los Angeles to bring out here for the pickers. They really were some fine people—as good as they come."

The Johnsons left unique records of their experiences with migrants. Photo-postcards that they made themselves were sent to pickers on the road, with friendly messages and passages from the Scriptures written on the back. "And they'd take films of people," an older woman remembered. "And whenever there was a night off, they'd show them. People would say, 'Hey! That's me!' and that film might have been taken a thousand miles away."

One reason the Johnsons are remembered so kindly is that they never judged pickers harshly. Bob remembered an encounter that was typical. "One time I came in from work, and it was so hot out, I thought, 'a cold beer sure would taste good.' So I got me one of them beers and I was settin' on the couch and there was a little space there between the couch and the wall where I

Right: *Postcards from missionaries in the 1940s.*
From the collection of Osie and Josephine Williams.

Dear Friends:

"They that wait upon the Lord shall renew their strength."

We have had a time of waiting upon the Lord, after the cotton picking till the pea harvest starts. We were a short time in Eloy with out services till this camp opened up, now we are again having services, and how good it seems to be giving forth His word once more and how God is blessing.

The picture shows some of the men around the fire in this camp, waiting for the peas to start, about the first of March. Our camp is located nine miles South West of Maricopa, on Papago Butte Ranch, at the end of Papago Road.

Yours for souls

Dear Friends:

"The eternal God is Thy refuge and underneath are the everlasting arms."

We at last arrived on the Islands after many delays and much testing. As we look at the camp we feel that God was surely in our move here, such an opportunity to give out the gospel, and what a need. Situated about five miles from Rio Vista across the ferry on Ryer Island the camp, composed of tents and trailers, is for pea pickers and will be dismantled after the harvest.

We wish we could be up in Idaho with our people as well as here. Much prayer is needed. Remember Sis. Johnson in her body.

In His service
Bro.&Sis.Johnson

had that beer. Well, Brother Johnson come along, and when he came in, I just shoved that beer back a little fer he wouldn't see it. And he says to me, 'Bob, you may as well go ahead and drink that beer while it's cold—it's no good once it's hot!' Boy, you sure couldn't slip anything by that old man." He paused and sighed, "I wish there were some people around like them nowadays."

Since people like the Johnsons no longer provide structure for the Okies' religious beliefs, there is little outlet for such faith. Without structured support and community pressure, religion becomes a more personal, individual choice. Many families become divided as women choose greater religious commitment, whereas men find it more dificult to abide by religious restrictions and prohibitions. But although people may disagree about their specific religious choices, their underlying belief system reflects many commonalities. Even those people who live outside of the religion for long periods of time and disregard religious prohibitions often view themselves as backsliders.

Ray, who was a Pentecostal preacher when his children were young, later left the religion because of philosophical differences. His own children viewed him as a backslider. After his oldest son became a preacher, Ray also came back to preaching.

Similarly, certain activities are judged by a religious moral code. Drinking and gambling, familiar activities among some groups of migrants, are commonly seen as a rejection of religion rather than simply a form of entertainment.

Okie migrants sometimes appear to scorn or make fun of their religious roots, but they are still tied to them, however loosely. Tommy, a young man who was married to one of Maxine's sisters, was known for his wild ways—drinking, driving fast cars, and gambling. After his marriage, he drifted in and out of the religion. Once when we were looking for the orchard where Gerald and Maxine were working, we saw him at another orchard. He was playing dice with some other pickers. "You

believe in that stuff, with those snakes and all?" he asked us. "I saw a rattler here the other day. I almost brought it up there to them so they could touch it!" he laughed. His manner was cynical and detached, yet when we saw him next it was at a church meeting, with his arm around his young son.

Although fruit pickers may drop many aspects of a strict religious upbringing, religious morality still pervades their thinking, determining their response to situations. In their work, they are more accepting and less likely to protest unfair conditions than less religious workers would be. "We believe the Lord will

Children get an early dose of right from wrong. Milton-Freewater, Oregon, 1977.

provide for us, so we don't worry about how much we make. We work because the Bible says, 'You shall work with your hands,' so we work with our hands," one of the more religious pickers explained. Although this is an extreme view, it helps to understand the Okies' casual acceptance of situations that might be intolerable to others.

Puritanical morals are a direct result of the religious upbringing. Although few people abide by the repressive rules of fundamentalist religion, most people still expect proper dress and conduct. In trying to pass their moral standards on to their children, Okies are sensitive to occurences in the camp that may reflect other standards. A girl wearing a halter top was frowned upon, and the women complained loudly. "If that was my daughter, I wouldn't let her walk around the camp that way."

Most migrants have a sense of propriety that allows for few variations. Babies are to be clothed, even on hot summer days, and women seldom breastfeed their babies, feeling that exposure of their breasts would be immoral. Parents keep a close eye on teenagers, and early marriages (girls may be as young as fifteen years) are encouraged to prevent sexual expression outside of marriage.

Small incidents sometimes illustrate the extremes of these strict moral codes. When Tommy Yancey saw his dog mating in the camp, with all the children watching, he was so upset by the incident that he took the dog away and shot it.

The pervasive religious morality survives even when other aspects of the religion do not. Popular evangelical interpretations such as the Moral Majority hold sway with many pickers as they try to make sense of their lives and what they believe. Although these beliefs conflict with the changing morality of the younger generation, the Okie migrant community is somewhat insulated from outside influences.

Ultimately, Okie fruit pickers must combine their life

A roll of the dice sometimes wins out over religion. Walla Walla, Washington, 1977.

experiences and their religious backgrounds to form their own set of values and beliefs. To this end, the strength of their religious upbringing may give them the courage to face the world

The Club, Cashmere, Washington, 1974.

that is changing around them. As one picker expressed it, "We've always lived the kind of life that was pleasing to God—whether to anybody else or not."

I Try to Give My Kids
Some Pride
The Children

11. "I Always Learned My Kids to Work"
Migrant Children at Work

"I'd want my kids working with me if we was making a million dollars an hour!" declared Mattie. For emphasis, she set her glass of iced tea down so hard on the table that the ice rattled.

We were visiting with Mattie and a group of other pickers in a trailer after work in a California orchard. The issue of child labor was on everybody's mind then, because the state Department of Labor had begun to enforce a previously inactive child labor law.

"I say, if the kids wanna work, let 'em," announced Clyde. On the opposite side of the dining booth, Clyde's large frame was sandwiched between the couch and the table. "It's not like when I

Left: *Cherry orchard ball team, Waterloo, California, 1974.*

was growing up, when you made fifty or seventy-five cents a day. I used to pick cotton for two and a half cents a pound. But my kids, they just got a real opportunity—they can go out there and make thirty, forty dollars a week. I wisht I'd had that opportunity when I was a kid."

"Yeah, I try to give my kids some pride in being a fruit picker," Bill nodded. He sat on the edge of a folding chair and sipped from a cup of coffee. "You know fruit-picker kids are really in demand on other jobs—they're fast, they're adaptable from having been in so many different places, and they're willing to work hard. Most kids nowadays are taught not to work, that it's not cool to work."

"That's right," agreed Bonnie from the trailer kitchen, where she poured another glass of iced tea. "When you see those kids in town, they turn bad a lot more than the kids in the fields. The kids in the fields are more responsible. They appreciate what they have more."

The enforcement of the child labor law in 1977, which prohibited children under twelve from working in the fields, met with strong reaction in Stockton, where thousands of fruit pickers had gathered for the cherry harvest. It was customary for these fruit-picking families to work together. "Child labor" was part of the cultural tradition of farm families, and to their way of thinking, it allowed parents to convey the values and skills of honest labor to their children and to maintain a strong spirit of family unity.

This family togetherness was also a major reason why many Okie families decided to stick with migrant farmwork. "That's one thing about this fruit tramping—you can really be close to your family," Marty told us. "If we lived in the city, we'd

Right: *"That's why I'm a fruit picker—it's the family unit."*
Milton-Freewater, Oregon, 1977.

both have jobs and we'd never see each other."

Even though his children are grown, Bill Taylor felt that the law marked the end of a cherished lifestyle.

When I heard about the child labor law, at first I didn't think much about it. I just thought—oh well, no kids in the field this year. But the next morning I got to thinking about it, and I just started crying. Because that's *why* I'm a fruit picker—it's the family unit. And for all these other old fruit tramps, it's the same way. We grew up this way, and it's the core of the family. Ever since I started picking fruit, there's been these big families from Arkansas and Oklahoma, picking fruit with all the kids. They won't be able to come out to pick now. This law means the end of our lifestyle and freedom is coming soon, and I hate to see it go.

Indeed many Okie fruit pickers left the migrant run after the enforcement of the child labor law in 1977 placed severe restrictions on their way of life. Others returned to California in subsequent years to work for growers who agreed to be lax about the law. Now they were more dependent than ever on the few growers who still allowed the families to work together. And their way of life was no longer simply misunderstood or discriminated against—now it had become illegal as well.

It was hard for me to understand the full impact of the California law in 1977 because we continued to work for a grower who allowed children in the fields long after our son was born in 1979. But in the summer of 1990, when I was picking cherries with my son—by then eleven years old, the state of Washington passed a similar law to apply the regulations of child labor to farm work, forbidding children under fourteen from working in the orchards.

I was shocked to think that my son could no longer work with me. Not only was it important to him financially, because he was saving for a new bike (one that we could not afford to buy

him otherwise), but it undermined my own core reasons for continuing to pick fruit. I suddenly found myself at odds with my liberal, nonmigrant friends as I tried to explain why working with my children in the summer was important to me. Worst of all, the law meant that this way of life—working together as a family—was really over for us and thousands of other fruit pickers. Even if I could find an employer who would overlook the regulations, we would still be engaging in a criminal violation of the law.

In the orchards where I worked, many of my co-workers were Hispanic now, and they, along with the younger Okie families, always worked with their children. What would they do now that the children couldn't work with them? If the women stayed home to care for the children, the single income would never support the family. And often there was no real home to stay at. If the family brought the children to day-care centers (none of

Cherry-box choo-choo, Stockton, California, 1974.

which were provided for at the time the law went into effect) they would lose more than the cost of the day care. They would lose the privilege of parenting their own children and much of the experience of daily life and work with them.

For nonmigrants, the child-labor question is a black-and-white issue. They see the need to protect children from overwork and exploitation. In contrast, many migrants view children in the fields as essential to a family-oriented work and lifestyle. A child's labor in the orchards may not be of financial value to the family for at least the first decade of life, but parents value their presence in other ways.

From the time the children are born they are brought out to the orchard where they spend their days in bassinets or blankets in the shade of a tree. Working close to the baby in the next tree, the mother or older sibling can attend to the baby whenever necessary. As the baby grows, the parents may bring a portable playpen and toys out to the field or simply let the older baby crawl on a blanket within sight of the parents. Toddlers become the most difficult to watch, here as anywhere, and older siblings or other older children in the field perform an invaluable service as baby-sitters.

Babies, toddlers, and young children receive much personal attention in the fields. As workers pass a bassinet or playpen in the orchard, they stop to talk to the baby. Other young children in the field come to play with the baby or toddler.

A new baby in the orchard is something special. Cove, Oregon, 1977.

Weaned from the nipple, ready for the bottle, Wenatchee Heights, Washington, 1978.

Although the first few years of a baby's life are stressful for the migrant mother because she is working full-time, carrying the baby and baby equipment through the field, and attending to the baby's needs, she is not isolated in her home, nor is she without support. The extended family system, which makes raising children the responsibility of many people instead of just the mother, is commonly seen in the fields. Family members often care for each other's children.

Even though we were not related to anyone we worked with, I often experienced the feeling of an extended family in the summer when we returned to pick fruit. Our son, Zak, was greeted by everyone, from young children to old people. They talked with him, joked with him, teased him, tickled and wrestled with him. He learned to be at ease with many different kinds of people, and to find familiarity with people rather than with objects or places. The people we picked fruit with were constant and familiar to him even though he saw them for only a short period of time each year. They remembered him from the time he was only six weeks old, when we first brought him to the cherry orchard. Like grandparents, they would remember funny stories about his toddler years to tell him years later.

One year when we returned to the cherry orchard in Lodi, California, where we regularly worked, we were greeted by a couple of older pickers who'd also worked there the year before. "We have your little boy's road grader," they said, producing the metal toy. "He must have forgot it last year. We thought we'd see you up in Wenatchee so we carried it up there, but we never did see you. So we just packed it around all winter." Zak went off with his old toy, delighted to have it back, while we thanked them profusely, amazed at both their concern and their faith that they would see us again.

Most Okie migrant parents firmly believe that their children should be taught to work from an early age. "I'd like to see

"If you don't teach your kid to work, how are they gonna learn?" Pasco, Washington, 1977.

my kids turn out to be responsible people and to know how to do something instead of just talking about it," one father commented. As opposed to mainstream culture, the Okies' culture places a high value on physical labor, which is often seen as more worthwhile than desk work.

Ronnie Martin, who traveled with his family from Arkansas each year to follow the cherry harvest, thought the child labor law was destructive to his family's values. "If you don't teach your kid how to work, how are they going to learn?" he asked. His son, aged fourteen, had picked cherries since he was five years old. "He's a born cherry picker," his father said proudly. But his mother pointed out that years of training had helped her son develop his skill on the job. "You can't just bring a fifteen-year-old into an orchard and expect him to know how to do it," she said.

At about three years of age, fruit-picker children are given buckets made from coffee cans or other containers so they can imitate adults' work—which is, at this age, their play. They are not expected to work much until the age of six or seven, when most children are expected to do a little real work every day. There are a few parents who cajole or bribe their children into working large segments of the day, but most parents accept that children of this age still need long periods of playtime. By the time children are about ten they are expected to work in earnest, and they are usually interested in having money of their own as well. By their early teens, children come close to the picking ability of adults and could support themselves if necessary. In a culture where many young adults marry early and have children of their own to support, such training and skills are seen as important and essential. It is the only inheritance their parents can afford to give them.

Migrant parents choose various ways of paying their children, often duplicating the relationship of a contractor to a crew. They may pay the younger children a flat daily or job wage, or a percentage per box, for example a dollar a box—or 50 percent of the wage. How much they are paid is a personal decision, but some of the usual factors that weigh in such a decision are the age of the child and his or her ability to handle all aspects of the job (moving and setting ladders, and so on). Since parents do, in effect, contract the job for their children, they expect that some of the child's wages are used for the living expenses of the family: food, shelter, gas, and other expenses. Smaller children often pick into their parents' boxes without

keeping track of the amount because it is too little to bother with. Older children can make quite a bit of money, and often preteens and teenagers will use their money toward expenses such as school clothes and bicycles.

Older pickers suggested to us that the work standards for migrant children have slackened. When we wondered why we couldn't find a child's size "Picker's Pal," the traditional metal cherry-picking bucket, we discovered that the company had stopped manufacturing that size bucket in 1983. Otis gave us his own version of why the small buckets were no longer being produced. "I guess they quit making those buckets for kids 'cause

Benton City, Washington, 1977.

"The kids in the fields are more responsible. They appreciate what they have more."

"Now all my boys can flat pick those cherries, and they pick 'em clean too," he boasted. "Especially that Floyd; he doesn't hardly get a leaf in his bucket."

the kids don't hardly work anymore. Floyd and Cathy sure don't make that boy of theirs work. It took him all mornin' to make a box the other day. When my boys were that age [five], they'd pick three, four boxes. They'd really work—well, I made 'em work. They'd start fightin' and I'd put a bucket on 'em and put 'em to work. Then when they got tired, I'd tell 'em to go sit on a box under a tree. Whenever they'd get to fightin' again, I'd just put 'em back to work."

"I always learned my kids to work," he continued. "I figured I wouldn't never have enough to help 'em when they was growed, so I give 'em a way to help themselves. If they wanted to sit under a tree and starve to death when they got older, well, that was their business."

Most children of Okie fruit pickers do attend school, although the families who migrate are often less consistent or reliable about attendance. Frequently migrants decide that it's not worth it to enroll their child in school for a couple of weeks, only to withdraw him or her when the family makes the next move.

Migrant education programs strive to give migrant children an opportunity to catch up to other school children, but migrants are often unaware or suspicious of such programs. "When I was in Florida, someone asked me, 'How do you like the migrant schools?'" a picker in Oregon told us. "And that was the first I ever heard of them. So I told him, 'I guess I don't like them too well since I never even heard of any such thing as a migrant school.' The only thing I can think of that my kids ever got from a migrant program was up in Washington, where they could get a free lunch."

Migrant programs tend to overlook white migrants because they are overwhelmed with the number of Hispanic migrant children in need of bilingual education. Within rural school systems both Hispanic and white migrants often suffer from prejudiced views held by teachers or other children. "I like going to school in Texas," said ten-year-old Angie, whose migrant family wintered in Texas, "But I don't like it up in Washington. All the students think they're hot shots."

Many permanent residents working in the school system own orchards or have family members who are orchard owners. Although they need migrants at harvest, they often see their impermanence as irresponsible and harmful to children. Frus-

trated by the inadequacies of the system in dealing with children who don't easily fit in, teachers and other school personnel rarely realize the difficulties that migrant families undergo to bring their children to school. A change of job locations can also represent a change in housing and school districts. Parents are hard-pressed to find the time to help their child integrate into a school system. Harvest working days are usually from dawn to dusk, and taking time off is rarely tolerated. And few migrant parents

Swimming in the irrigation canal, Stockton, California, May 1975.

Left: *"They've been raised to pick fruit and they don't know nothin' else." Benton City, Washington, 1977.*

are skilled at negotiating the clash of cultural values that often occurs when the child goes to school.

Walter remembered the feeling that migrants were outcasts when he grew up. "They used to have this thing where, bein' as the public school didn't want to have any migrant kids in it, they'd open separate schools away from town, out by where the work was. We took advantage of it and probably attended school a lot more because it was right near us. And we thought it was really fun 'cause it was our school. But we didn't realize that we were bein' segregated and pushed out of the public schools 'cause they didn't want us."

Despite attempts to remedy such inequities in the public school system, migrant children still have trouble integrating into the schools. Many migrant parents did not complete elementary school, so from their perspective, the education that their children receive is extensive. "Most of the people in their forties and fifties now, who were migrant workers when they were growing up, would have got something like a sixth- to ninth-grade education," commented Daniel, "whereas a lot of them now are gettin' into high school and a good lot of them are finishing high school."

His brother Walter agrees, "I think a whole lot of migrant people are receiving a better education now than they were years ago. Kids are realizin' that it takes more than just bein' able to read and write to get by in this society, so they're gettin' educations."

Unfortunately, many migrant teens do not finish high school. The frequent moves put them at a disadvantage compared to other students. Floyd Brown, who was then working in Lodi, California, described with regret his children's past year in various schools. "My kids started out school in Selah [Washington], then we moved to Porterville [California], then they went to school in Arkansas, and now here. They changed schools four

Angie, Kennewick, Washington, 1977.

Okanogan, Washington, October 1978.

times. Just when they'd get to feelin' like they really belonged, it'd be time to go again. They didn't like it much. I ain't gonna do that to them again. I told them that wherever they start out next year, we're gonna stay there."

By high school, many migrant students are a year behind other students because of the frequent changes of schools and missed attendance. Also by the time they are in high school, they are able to earn a decent living picking fruit. They've absorbed much practical information about cars and trailers and are capable of owning their own home—a trailer—and caring for it. Many fruit-picker teens are raising their families well before the age of eighteen, and they see little reason to continue their education.

These children who grow up and continue to follow the fruit are used to a life of hard work and responsibility. One picker told us he'd compared these young adults in the orchard with kids he knew who weren't raised to work. "Those kids just laid around their apartment playing Nintendo. They took odd jobs and lived off the money their parents send them in between. I'd think about how different they were from fruit-picker kids. Like these Rogers kids we worked next to in Lodi. They were only twenty and they had babies and cars and trailers and they'd worked to earn all of that. They're so *responsible*. And they're so enthusiastic about the work. They run all the time. Nothing gets them down—if they have bad picking they just get right through it—they have so much energy!"

The children of Okie fruit pickers are raised by old-fashioned standards. Girls are expected to care for younger children and do domestic chores. Although boys are given greater leeway and allowed to go swimming or for a drive after work, the girls must frequently stay home to do housework or baby-sit. They are expected to marry young, and they are watched more closely than the boys. When Esther was fifteen and sixteen, she was not allowed to go out on dates—yet by the time she was eighteen she was teased about being an old maid because she didn't have a steady boyfriend.

"Fruit-picker kids grow up quicker, they get married young, and they mature fast." Flathead Lake, Montana, 1978.

"Fruit-picker kids grow up quicker, they get married young, and they mature fast," a parent explained to us proudly.

Walter revealed the differences in the way he raised his six children as he told us how he planned to help his oldest son get a new pickup when he graduated from high school. "I figure I'll help the boys get started out. The girls'll need to marry someone good to provide for them." He thought a moment. "Unless they're different," he added. "Making exception for these days of women's liberation and all that."

Because early marriage is the norm, teenage romances invite speculation and talk of marriage in the camp. When Elvie, aged sixteen, became involved with seventeen-year-old Bonnie, everyone teased him relentlessly. Mattie, Elvie's mother, saw him looking at engagement rings in town. She told her husband Walter, "You better have a long talk with that next-to-oldest son of ours." But Walter dismissed it, saying, "Every boy from the age of nine looks at engagement rings."

The situation developed day by day, with everyone in camp aware of all the details. On the day Bonnie's family was about to leave for another job, her mother gave Elvie's parents the names of people to work for in Bridgeport where they worked. "My daughter will be awful unhappy if Elvie don't come up there," Bonnie's mother said. Later in the evening, she told Mattie that Bonnie had never met anyone she liked as well as Elvie. She was a preacher, she told Mattie, and could marry them right in the orchard.

Mattie was fuming. "That boy can't get married without his mama's signature, and I ain't signin'!"

At that point Walter began to take it more seriously too and said he'd have to have a talk with Elvie. "I want him to finish high school before he thinks about getting married. He can write her all winter and then if he still likes her, they can talk marriage next year."

Bonnie's family left for their next job and Elvie's family went elsewhere to work. Although they saw each other again that season, their families didn't live in the same camp. Things tapered off, and they didn't marry after all.

Through moving to certain jobs and avoiding others, parents can exert control over their teenage children's ro-

Stemilt Hill, Washington, 1976.

mances. Other times, they find amusement in the perplexities of such migratory romances. Doris spoke laughingly of her son's quandary: "He really liked this one little gal on Rodney's crew, but they were just friends, you know. Then he started goin' with a gal in Kennewick and now he's afraid that both of these gals will be on the job in Quincy! He's skeered he'll have them both mad at him!"

Migrants who remember the discrimination they grew up with as children can only hope for something better for their own children, but at the same time they struggle to maintain dignity for the work they do. Walter tried to describe to us the pervasive sense of shame that he felt as a child. "Well, when I grew up I was made to feel that being a fruit picker was the most low-down thing a person could be. A service-station attendant or a garbage collector was way better than a fruit tramp. It's hard to describe it, but you felt it all the time. It was drummed into my head that I was just a sorry human being.

"I remember when I was sixteen, I had a big fight with my father," Walter continued. "I wanted to stay in Porterville, and I told him I wasn't going up north that year. Oh, we had a big fight and the whole basis for it was, he said that I was tryin' to be better than him. And that just drummed it into my head even more, that fruit picking was the sorriest thing in the world."

Walter, who returned to fruit picking determined to make it work to be proud of, is convinced that his children don't have to experience such shame. "Kids now have it a lot better, and there's none of them that ever have to feel that they're sorry or low down," he concluded.

But Walter's son, Elvie, believes that an education could bring him better employment. "I'd like to be either a lawyer or an auto mechanic. I'm not gonna pick fruit after I'm out of high

school. Daddy always said he wanted something better for us kids."

Other fruit pickers are aware that their children still suffer from the prejudices of the surrounding communities. "Twenty years ago there was a lot of poor people around—in the houses near the migrant camps—they were on the same level with the migrant workers," Darlene explained. "Now you'll be in a camp and the people in the houses nearby won't allow their children to play with the fruit-picker children."

Bill reflected on how such prejudices had affected his grown son. "My son didn't make it out this year. There's something that goes with cherry picking, kind of a social stigma. My kids picked up on that. Whenever we'd go to Flathead Lake and they'd meet girls, they'd tell 'em they were on vacation. Then they'd ask, 'Well, where'd you go all day?' and one lie would lead to another. The kids wouldn't want to say they'd been picking cherries." Bill paused. "There's a price to doin' this," he said thoughtfully.

Despite the stigma of fruit picking, many migrant parents believe that the migrant way of life is a good way to raise children. "People say that the life of a picker ain't much. I agree, things could be a helluva lot better. But I got what many people want, what they can't afford. And that's the freedom to go where I want, when I want. I got six kids born in six different states. Geography ain't something they have to learn from a textbook. It's something they experience every day of their lives."

Because migrating is a fact of life for these children, traveling is often in their blood even after they are grown. "Whatever my son does decide to do, he'll have a hard time stayin' in one place," commented one migrant father. "Once someone's

Left: *Orchard rummy game, Kennewick, Washington, 1976.*

152 / The Children

seen the mountains and the deserts, they just can't stay settled in one place."

Some parents worry about what sort of future their children can look forward to. They know that they are passing skills and adaptations to their children that will no longer be valued or useful when their children are grown. "When we started working, you could go anywhere and get a job," Ruby said. "Now it's getting hard to find work. What I really wonder about is the family—the kids and the grandkids. What'll they do? They've been raised to pick fruit and they don't know nothin' else. My grandson is thirteen and he can pick fifteen or twenty boxes a day—now, that's a pretty good day's wages. But I don't know what he'll do when he can't find a job in the fruit."

Left: *"What I wonder about is the family—the kids and the grandkids." Cashmere, Washington, 1981.*

12. "I Wish Ma Was Here to Talk To"
Children Returning to the
Fruit Run

In the afternoon after cherry picking one day, I was cleaning our trailer and half-heartedly preparing dinner, still groggy from a short nap. It was about five o'clock when an unfamiliar orange pickup with a camper on the back drove into the camp. A woman got out and walked up to our trailer. I opened the door and was so startled to see Esther's familiar face that for a moment I couldn't recognize her.

I'd known Esther from the time she was twelve. We worked with her parents, Walter and Mattie Williams, in Florida, California, and Washington and had come to know the family intimately. Esther and I had shared talks and confidences

Left: *Milton-Freewater, Oregon, 1977.*

through her teenage years. But because her family had stopped coming west regularly to pick fruit, I hadn't seen Esther in several years. Now here she was—twenty-one years old, married, and a mother.

Contrasting with Esther's sharp, bony features, her husband Duane had a rotund shape and a pudgy, adolescent-looking face. Esther, Duane, and another friend, John, came into our small trailer, sipping Pepsi through straws in jumbo-sized cups. We talked for awhile and Esther told us that a group of them— five adults and four children—had come out from Texas together to try to make some money picking fruit. None of them had ever picked before except Esther. She had been trying to find the group of them a job, without much success. "We went up to the Heights but Bud ain't starting for another three days. The Yanceys are supposed to be camped down the road from here, so that'll be somewheres for us to stay 'til our job starts. Do ya think they'd put anyone on here where ya'all work?"

Obligingly, Rick went off to find the foreman and ask him about jobs for Esther and her crew. Meanwhile, Esther asked me if I wanted to see her baby. She led me around to the back of the camper and opened the door. Inside there were two young women about her age sitting on a small couch and three toddlers playing on the floor. One of the women handed the baby to Esther. "He's been spittin' up," she said. "I've been giving him juice but he won't hold it down."

Esther took the crying baby outside and handed him to me. I put his head on my shoulder and walked with him. Suddenly bright green vomit cascaded onto my hair and clothes. Esther quickly took the baby back, apologizing. "I don't know what's the matter with him. I guess I better take him down to that migrant clinic. Do you know where it is?"

As I wiped the vomit off my clothes, I gave Esther directions to the clinic. Rick came walking back with the news. "Well,

Okanogan picker's cabin, Washington, 1978.

it looks like they're full up. He says he's got more pickers than he can handle right now."

Esther tilted a bottle full of bright pink fluid into the baby's mouth. "Well, I reckon we'd better be goin' and see if we can find the Yanceys," she said. "Ya'all come up and see us in a couple days, up on the Heights."

As we waved good-bye to the crowded truck, I wondered uneasily how Esther would do on the fruit run. It can be tough for children of fruit pickers who return to work alone or with others who haven't grown up in the migrant life. When the children marry other pickers, they tend to continue leading a migratory life with ease. But children who marry nonmigrants become isolated from their extended families as they become part of the larger society—and coming back can be fraught with problems.

On a hot, sultry day in July we quit work early and decided to take a drive to see Esther. The heat softened as we climbed the road up to Wenatchee Heights, leaving the fiery hot valley. Our truck passed orchards, pastures with horses, and undeveloped desert land. At the top of the hill, we could see the valley below with neat squares and rectangles of green orchard dotted with buildings between the arid browns and lavenders of desert ground.

We turned down Jagla Road past lush cherry orchards, the tree limbs laden with ripe fruit. In one of those orchards there was a small and clean pickers' camp—three or four trailers shining with unpaid-for newness and a tent or two. We got out of the car to talk to the residents. Two of the families were related to friends of ours, older pickers who have now retired because of various ailments, leaving their children to carry on the work.

Linda, appearing from her sparkling new trailer, didn't look much like her mother, Hazel, but reminded me of her with her warmth and hospitality. In her midthirties, with short-cropped dark hair, she was clad in a pink halter top and blue jeans. "C'mon inside, Toby," she urged. "I'm just trying to finish the supper." She dragged out boxes of toys for my three-year-old to play with and continued talking as she cooked in the trailer kitchen.

Since Linda's parents started picking after she was married, she never worked with them as a family, and this was only her second year of fruit picking. She was unhappy and discouraged with cherry picking and complained bitterly about the rigors of the work, the lack of privacy, the other people in the camp, and her husband's increased drinking. "Lord, I wish Ma was here to talk to!" she groaned. "Does everybody on this fruit run drink? I'd like to go back home but we sold our house before we left, so this is all the home in the world I got now. Darn, I just ain't no cherry picker!"

As she talked, Linda stirred the spaghetti sauce, supervised her four-year-old son, and bantered with her teenage son

Older fruit-picker children are raised to care for younger ones. Walla Walla, Washington, 1977.

and the younger sister and brother who were temporarily staying with her. Kevin, her twenty-one-year-old brother, was going back to his parents in Oregon the next day. "Well, I told Kevin, he's done pretty well—he don't have much money but he got a new pair of boots and a watch and a lot of clothes. It's better'n we've done, I'm tellin' ya!"

Linda's husband Dave walked in then, complaining about the heat and adjusting the air conditioner. He opened the refrigerator and pulled out a beer. "That's the third one you've had this afternoon," Linda complained.

"These are just small ones," he protested. "What's for dinner?"

"Spaghetti," Linda answered and immediately everyone groaned. "Spaghetti!" Linda's sister exclaimed. "I wanted a hamburger."

"Well, you'll just have to make it yourself," Linda retorted.

Rick entered the trailer then, and asked, "Do you know where Esther and her group are? We thought they'd be over here."

"Oh, no," Linda replied. "They're over at that other camp. Esther and that crazy bunch of kids pulled in here one afternoon and they couldn't figure out how to get that camper off their truck. I guess they didn't have any jacks or nuthin' so they just tied the camper to a tree and drove off. That camper landed with a big thud on the ground—I never seen nothin' like it! Then they took off to town and Bud, the farmer, came by and got mad about that camper bein' over here—they was supposed to park it over in the other camp. So he winched it up on his flatbed truck and pulled it over to the other orchard, tied it to a tree, and snapped it off. He said he figured, if they was gonna do it, so was he."

We got directions to the other camp and said goodbye to Linda and Dave. "Maybe we'll see you up there in Montana," said Dave. "We called up there to that Staves job and if we get done with this one soon enough, we'll go on up."

Our truck wound around the country roads until we reached a dusty road through an orchard. The scorching heat of the afternoon assaulted us again as we neared the other camp. The road was punctuated with potholes, filled with water from rain the day before. Suddenly a tent appeared, then an old bus with the paint peeling off, and on the other side of the road,

When fruit pickers marry other pickers, they often raise their children on the fruit run. Kennewick, Washington, 1979.

View from Stemilt Hill, Washington, 1974.

another tent and camper. Skinny tow-haired kids ran through the puddles of water, yelling and splashing. In the middle of the road, people sat on lawn chairs, smoking and talking, drinking beer and soda pop. Sweat rolled down their gaunt, leathery faces, and they waited until our truck was almost upon them before they looked up. Then they moved their chairs slowly, reluctantly, just enough so we could barely squeeze by.

Beyond this obstacle course, we saw more trailers and tents. Earl and Linette's modern, thirty-foot tip-out trailer looked out of place among the older, run-down vehicles and trailers.

In back of the camp, we saw Esther and Duane's camper lying flat on the orchard grass. There was a group of people sitting on lawn chairs and cherry buckets in front of Earl and Linette's trailer, and Earl beckoned to us to join them. He leaned back against his trailer. On his right side were a man and a woman we hadn't met before. They looked hard, with tanned faces and hands weathered and aged beyond their years. On Earl's left side were Esther and Duane, jiggling their baby in a stroller. Linette appeared from the trailer to say hello to us and cooed to the baby for a few minutes before she disappeared inside again.

We weren't introduced to the couple we didn't know, and their conversation resumed as if it were never interrupted. Their talk focused on complaints and disappointments about the job and the way it was run.

"You know, those folks in the other orchard are kind of personal friends of Bud's, and they get all the gravy," said Earl bitterly. "We're just supposed to go in after them and clean up what they don't want."

"Yeah, today we didn't even work, and that other crew was out there working all day!" said the woman. "He said there wasn't enough ripe for all of us to pick."

"I'm tellin' you, it gets worse every year," Earl continued. "I don't believe I've made my gas money up from Texas yet. Used to be, I'd quit a job like this, but now there ain't much else to choose from!"

We asked Esther how she was getting along, and she shook her head grimly. Worry lines were already etched into her forehead. "Terrible," she replied. "Everybody started complaining about how little we were making and how hard it was, and I've been doing all the tops of the trees myself. And we'd buy food—fifty dollars' worth of food—and it'd be gone the next day, and they wouldn't buy any more food. So we started tellin' 'em they couldn't eat our food, and they got mad and said we couldn't use their truck. They wouldn't even give us a ride into town to buy food. And then the baby got real sick, and they wouldn't let us use the truck, so we had to walk to town. We walked all the way down that hill, ten miles, in the middle of the night, to get him to the hospital. He's okay now, but he was in there two days. And all we've been able to save so far is a hundred dollars and we need to buy a truck so we can get that camper back home to Texas, 'cause they won't take it for us."

The baby started crying, and Esther picked him up, bouncing him nervously while he continued to cry. Finally she handed him to Duane, who held him awkwardly and talked self-consciously to him.

My own son was requiring attention by then, tugging at my arm and pulling me. It was time for us to leave. "Well, we better head back to town and get something to eat," Rick said.

"Eat!" Earl exclaimed. "Boy, you must be making a lot of money. You better not talk about food—none of us can afford to eat," he joked wryly.

As we drove back down that long hill into the thick warm air of the valley, the contrast of the two camps was still sharp in my mind. I wondered what would happen to Esther and her family after the job ended, stranded ten miles from the nearest town with no vehicle or money. Without the support of her large extended family, she seemed so alone and so burdened by responsibilities.

Much later that summer, we heard that Esther and Duane had sold the camper for next-to-nothing and bought a decrepit hundred-dollar car. Earl drove his own truck and trailer with them all the way back to Texas, stopping often to repair their car. Then, after visiting with Esther's parents and other friends in Texas, Earl and Linette headed back to California and Washington for more picking.

Right: *Mother and son, Brewster, Washington, 1977.*

Far Right: *Pasco, Washington, 1978.*

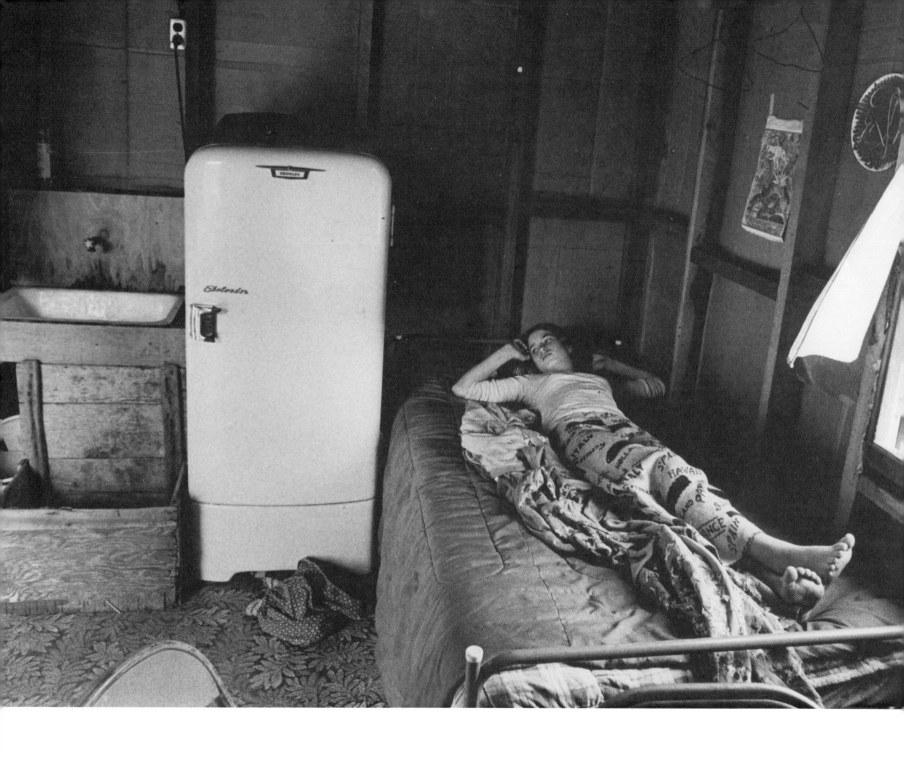

13. "There's a Lot of People Who've Had It Happen to Them"
When the Children Are Taken Away

The very act of raising children on the migrant fruit run is fraught with controversy. On the one hand, our culture professes to uphold individual choice and autonomy, strengths of the migrant workers' life; on the other hand societal norms about what is good for children are based on values and cultural preconceptions that sharply contrast with the values of the Okie migrants. Their choices as parents, far from being intimate family matters, open them up to criticism by schools and state institutions and leave them vulnerable to losing the privilege of raising their own children.

Left: *Angie, Okanogan, Washington, 1978.*

Although such a sensitive subject is rarely discussed by migrants who have suffered such an experience, one time we did have such a conversation with R. J. and Betty. We were returning from the grocery store to the camp in our car with R. J. and Betty in the back seat between the piles of grocery bags.

"Seems like it takes twenty dollars a day to feed my family, no matter what we eat," R. J. said. "So we might as well eat meat as eat beans."

"Well, I guess I can cook a good pot of beans anyway," commented Betty. "I cooked nearly two hundred pounds of 'em last winter. We bought two of those hundred-pound sacks down there in Milton-Freewater. This year I'd sure like to get a different flavor!"

R. J. laughed. "You know, when I was a kid and we used to go through these towns, I used to think that no person in a settled community or living in any kind of house at all would ever eat any such thing as a bean!" he told us, with a tinge of bitterness in his voice. "I thought they were all rich, and it was only us migrants that were poor."

"Well, one of these days when our kids is all growed and gone away, it won't cost us so much to eat," Betty commented. "But then I reckon we won't know how to cook for just the two of us!"

Everyone was silent for a few minutes, and the light mood changed as we turned off the highway and onto the back road toward Lodi, passing cherry orchards, walnut groves, and vineyards. My thoughts turned towards Leroy, R. J.'s cousin who had had two of his children taken away from him by the sheriff and placed in a juvenile home several days ago. Since the incident, it had been a major topic for speculation and concern around the camp but we hadn't discussed it yet with R. J. and Betty.

Rick brought it up first. "Have you heard much about what happened with Jenny and Sara? Was Leroy really beating them?" he asked.

"Well, he just gave them a whuppin', no worse than what we give our kids!" Betty said. "And it was on account of those people livin' next to 'em, they was tryin' to get the kids to run away with them, to work for them, so they're the ones who called the sheriff and told him Leroy was beatin' up on the kids."

"Yeah, they saw what good workers they were and thought they could just adopt them as sort of a free work force," R. J. added. "But all Leroy was doin' was warmin' their bottoms

Milton-Freewater, Oregon, 1977.

to teach them a lesson. Now, I wouldn't defend the way he treated those girls. He could be pretty mean to them. He just went too far. After they took those girls away, Leroy came to me and he was in tears, saying he'd tried as hard as he could but he just couldn't make a good father. You see, after Leroy and his wife split up, Leroy took the kids and started following the fruit run. But before that, those kids had spent their whole life in Arkansas, going to school, having friends there, and doing whatever they wanted. And they didn't like having to work [on the fruit run] and live with Jackie [Leroy's common-law wife]."

R. J. became quiet and introspective for several minutes. Then he began talking about the painful time years ago when his own children were taken away. For as long as we'd known them, R. J. and Betty had been surrounded by their noisy, active brood of five children.

But there was a time when things were different. The family had finished the apple harvest in Washington and was headed down to California when their youngest child got sick. Since they were traveling, they wanted to wait until they reached California before taking her to a doctor. But by the time they got her to a hospital she had a bad case of pneumonia. Betty's relatives, angry at them for being fruit pickers and "not keeping up with the Joneses" as R. J. says, turned them in for child neglect. Then followed a long ordeal of trying to prove themselves to be good parents so they could get the kids back. R. J. tried going on the fruit run to get money for a pickup and camper for the family but the agency didn't approve.

"They said they wanted me to get all settled down and to quit the fruit run," R. J. explained, "so we got an apartment in town and got on welfare, and they liked that real good. They said we was doin' fine, just keep it up! Then we bought us a new Dodge van and a twenty-one-foot trailer on payments, and they were really happy. They raised my welfare payments. But there

Father's Day, Okanogan, Washington, 1978.

was no way in the world even then that I could make the payments in the winter. But I figured I had four months before they would take it away, and I could go on the fruit run again.

"The worst thing those guys ever done was when they sent me a letter saying I had to pay for the foster homes to take care of my kids!" R. J. remembers angrily. "Those guys really had a lot of gall! The way they put it, they said that if I paid it would show that I really cared for my kids and if I didn't, it showed I didn't care at all. I told them it was like hanging you and making you buy the rope to hang you from. I said I'd pay to take care of my kids when they were living with me, and since they took them away, they should pay for them."

Implicit in such incidents is the condemnation of the migratory life. Whether turned in by fellow pickers, resentful relatives, outsiders, or agencies, migrant families are easy targets for criticism. R. J. directly confronted such prejudice. "I told them I wasn't going to stop picking fruit. It was an honorable occupation and there wasn't a thing wrong with it. The lawyer we had there, he told us that there was nothing on the books that said you couldn't be a fruit picker, but as soon as you got into a brush with the law, it was illegal to be a fruit picker," R. J. said angrily.

"There's a lot of people who've had it happen to them," he continued, "but it doesn't get talked about. You won't never hear about it. People will say, 'The kids are at the relatives' or something. People feel so bad about it, so guilty, they don't want to see anyone. When it happened to us, we'd walk across the street just so we wouldn't have to talk to a real good friend of ours, and we'd just pretend we didn't hear him when he hollered."

"I guess maybe that's why Leroy left—he just didn't wanna talk to nobody," Betty said, returning to the subject of Leroy' daughters. After they'd been taken away, Leroy and the rest of his family left without telling anyone that they were leaving or where they were going. Everyone in camp had been upset that he'd left before the court case. "He won't have no chance of winning them back now," Pauline had claimed. "The courts will say he deserted them kids, leaving like that."

R. J. explained Leroy's behavior to us. "Well, I know how he felt. It was like he had already lost the girls and he didn't want to lose the other kids."

Our car turned into the gravel driveway of the pickers' camp, and our conversation ended abruptly. R. J. and Betty's children clamored around the car, wanting to know what goodies awaited them and helping to carry the bags inside.

Turning from these bright and energetic children, I watched all the activity around us in the camp. There were children everywhere: riding bikes on the dirt roads, climbing trees, running through the orchard sprinklers, or swimming in

The lifestyle makes them easy targets for criticism. Okanogan, Washington, 1978.

Right: *Okanogan, Washington, 1978.*

the irrigation canals. Their parents watched them and slowly tried to gather them inside for bed.

Across the wire fence that separated the orchard from the suburban community, children played on in the playgrounds of their spacious backyards, calling to each other in the twilight. Their family life was private, taking place inside a house that provided a soundproof, secluded barrier from the rest of the world.

Wenatchee Heights, Washington, 1978.

In contrast, family life in a pickers' camp is open for all to see, and privacy is a rare commodity. Trailers, campers, and tents are so small and so warm in the summer that much time is spent outdoors. The trailers are parked close together and sounds pass easily through the paper-thin walls. Though migrant adults are free to live as they choose, the same is not true for migrants with children. Open to public view and social criticism, they must be very cautious and very lucky to avoid being torn apart from their families.

It Was Drummed into My Head
That I Was a Sorry Human Being
Migrants and Society

14. "We're a Part of Feeding These People Who Have This Contempt for Us"
Migrants and the Community

One evening, after the children in camp were asleep for the night, a few people still sat outside in the waning light of dusk, quietly talking. The screen door of one of the trailers nearby opened with a creak, and a woman poked her head out.

"Hank, would you run to the store for some bread?" We ain't got enough for tomorrow's lunch."

Hank sighed and got up from his chair reluctantly. "That's about the third time today I've been up at that there Tom's Market," he complained. "I swear, those people are gettin' rich off us fruit tramps."

Left: *East Wenatchee, Washington, 1974.*

As he headed for his pickup, the other pickers watched him sympathetically. The little store he was driving to, only a mile and a half away, was surrounded by orchards and used mainly by pickers who didn't want to travel five miles to a larger town.

Walter shook his head. "Yeah, I bought three dollars of groceries over there today, and the man only charged me five dollars!" he quipped.

"Well, you know they jack the prices up just as soon as the fruit pickers hit town," Darlene said. "A gallon of milk is thirty cents higher once the pickers get into town. They just figure we got no choice."

"What gets me is the way some of these locals act toward you, like your money ain't as good as theirs." Travis, a small, energetic man, wrinkled his forehead in disgust. "I went into the grocery one time, and I'd been uptown and got me sixty-five dollars worth of food stamps in my pocket. And I'm about to pay for my groceries, when this old lady says to me, 'You'd better go to the back of the line.' I said, 'Why is that?' and she said, 'Those food stamps. I had to pay for those things.' I said, 'Lady, I had to pay for 'em too, and I got every right to 'em.' Hell, I bet that old lady was drawin' her social security too!

"That makes me so blame mad!" he went on. "We're the ones that's harvesting their food and they think they're better'n us just because we have to use food stamps when there ain't no work."

Because most of the interactions between migrants and the community occur in stores, especially grocery stores, these are the main places where each group forms its opinion of the other. Most of the Okies we talked to had an active distrust of store-keepers. We never discovered if the stores really raised their prices when the pickers came to town, but many of the people we worked with believed they did. Smaller markets, which fruit pickers must often rely on because they are more rural, always had higher prices than stores in town, because of various economic factors. Because pickers frequented these stores in such great numbers, they often felt that they were being taken advantage of because of their needs.

Pear Wash, Cashmere, Washington, 1988.

Right: *"You know how when they give you your change back, whenever you got dirty hands from workin' in the fields, they hold their hand six or eight inches from yours and drop your money down into it." Kennewick, Washington, 1974.*

Fruit pickers are especially sensitive to the attitudes of grocery-store clerks. They often feel negatively judged for the work they do—yet this is the very work that the grocery business profits from.

"Those storekeepers look down on us fruit tramps," Darlene told us. Her strong voice had a bitter edge. "You know how when they give you your change back, whenever you got dirty hands from workin' in the fields, they hold their hand six or eight inches from yours and drop your money down into it."

"Yeah," agreed Thelma, a mild-mannered woman who was married to Travis. "Or they lay the money on the counter, like they'd catch something awful if they touched you."

This particular experience of the clerk not putting the change in the fruit picker's hand is one I heard complaints of often, and I experienced it personally. The implication that fruit pickers are too dirty to touch is especially damaging to a picker's pride.

"It's always been that-a-way," commented Daniel, Darlene's husband, trying to explain the phenomenon. "The people in the towns always seem to get the idea that fruit pickers are dirty. Because they may work ten or fifteen miles off from where they live, and rather than to come home and clean up and then go to the store and buy something for the next day's lunch or supper that night, they just stop on the way home. It saves havin' to go back to town. I guess you could call it conservation of energy, but we seem to have gotten an unclean reputation from doin' this."

Fruit pickers must also use stores more frequently because of their limited storage space and refrigeration. Often there are no sanitary facilities in the field, so their hands as well as their clothes can be dirty from contact with fruit, trees, and ladders. Their hands are torn, covered with hundreds of scratches and cuts from the trees. They are tired, hungry, and dirty by the time they come to the store to buy their food and spend their hard-earned money. If the attitude of the grocery-store clerk is hostile, the experience is not soon forgotten.

"For some reason or other, seems like the communities have a poor outlook on migrants," said Daniel's older brother, Walter. With deep lines etched into his face, Walter looked much older than his forty years. Unlike Travis and Daniel, who wore crisply ironed western shirts with blue jeans, Walter's clothes were rumpled and old, as if he had no time for such frivolities as dress. His demeanor was serious and thoughtful as he continued. "I think local people figure we don't have roots or aren't a part of anything. When in reality, we do have roots, very strong roots, and we are a part of something. We're a part of feeding these people who have this contempt for us."

John Steinbeck noted this same contradiction in *Their Blood Is Strong* in 1938. "Thus, in California we find a curious attitude toward a group that makes our agriculture successful,"

Brewster, Washington, 1978.

he wrote. "The migrants are needed, and they are hated. . . . They are never received into a community nor into the life of a community. Wanderers in fact, they are never allowed to feel at home in the communities that demand their services."[1]

Migrants feel that they contribute to the economics of the community not only by their work but by the money they spend locally. "You know, this thing about not spending any money in the community is an absolute lie." said Thelma. "Our cars break down and we get 'em worked on; we buy lots of food and gas and other things too when the job is good and pay for a place to stay lots of times."

The perception that they are taken advantage of by the communities they frequent extends to other services that fruit pickers rely on. "We put five hundred dollars into that truck of ours and you wouldn't believe it," Linda related acridly. "All in this little part that fell off, and this crook in Othello charged us an arm and a leg cuz he knew we couldn't get out of that nasty little town without it. I think I would've left and run away back home if I had a home to run to."

In addition to grocery stores, car-repair places, gas stations, and campgrounds, migrants use state or community services for health care. Because of a disinclination to use such services as well as the difficulty of obtaining regular health care on the migrant run, such services are usually used only for a health crisis, and preventative health care is rarely sought out by migrants. Cultural factors add to the Okies' reluctance to seek health care. A suspicion of medical practitioners; a belief that they can often cure themselves (or a more fatalistic belief that they were meant to be sick); and denial of all but the most major illness, combined with a strong work ethic, all contribute to this behavior.

Left: *Elvie, Okanogan, Washington, 1978.*

Kennewick, Washington, 1976.

culty of eating well. In addition, few fruit pickers pay attention to or are educated about the latest nutritional theories. The Okie diet often includes meals that combine meat (frequently pork), cornbread or biscuits, a canned or frozen vegetable, and a sweet dessert. In times of good work and larger paychecks, fruit pickers commonly indulge in fast-food snacks such as chips, candy, and soda pop.

Low standards of hygiene and diet for migrants may be balanced with the health benefits of hard, physical work outdoors with their families. Pickers don't seem to succumb to sickness more often than the mainstream population, but they have more difficulty obtaining medical care and more reservations about using the medical care available. Migrants who seek medical care generally have serious health problems and are often in real pain. They are frequently unhappy with the treatment they receive.

"The stores ain't the only ones that'll treat you bad," said Travis. "I went into that Linden Migrant Clinic one time about my arm, and that doctor really got smart-alecky with me. He said, 'Take a hot-water bottle and put it on there, and if you don't have a hot-water bottle, just take one of your old wine bottles and set it out in the sun all day and sleep on it.'"

"I've had a hard time with some of these doctors too," Ruby concurred. "I got bit by a black wider spider in the orchard once, and I went to the doctor and he looked at me and said, 'When's the last time you changed your mattress? I believe you have bedbugs!' I told him I knew I didn't have bedbugs because I'd slept on the same bed in the camper for five years and it was clean! But he gave me the treatment for them and I went home and I was gettin' sicker and sicker 'til I finally went back to the hospital."

"That really gripes me!" said Darlene. A young mother of six, she is quick to anger at any injustice. "Them hospitals is

Poor personal hygiene and diet can lead to a need for medical services. Personal hygiene among migrants is often inadequate because of the lack of water and adequate sanitary facilities in the fields. For example, pickers often eat their meals in the field without washing their hands, which are dirty and also carry the residue of pesticides. Children and adults alike eat fruit from the trees without washing it, for the same reasons. There is seldom any water for pickers to wash their hands after using an orchard outhouse.

The diet of fruit pickers tends to be of low quality as well. Feeding large families on a small budget contributes to the diffi-

really bad for lettin' fruit pickers wait around too. I was there with my leg impacted, in a wheelchair, and I felt like I was about to die, and they let me sit there four hours before they so much as took a look at me!"

Thelma nodded as she listened to Darlene's tale. "This one time when we was workin' in Salem, our boss's wife hurt herself and she went down to the county hospital and she told me, 'I thought they were never gonna treat me. They must have thought I was a fruit picker.' I said, 'What do they do around here, let the fruit pickers die?' Then she realized she'd said something wrong and she said, 'Some people sure act funny, don't they?' I said, 'They sure do!' That made me so mad!"

Prenatal care is sadly lacking among Okie migrant women. Few of them seek care in early pregnancy, both because they think they don't need to and because they know they will soon be in a different location. Several women told me they were unable to see doctors in late pregnancy because they hadn't started out with them. Even migrant clinics are sometimes limited in the care they can provide. When Darlene went to see a doctor at the Agricultural Workers Clinic in Linden, California, she was told that the clinic for pregnant women was only on Wednesday nights and they couldn't see her any other time, even though she was leaving the area before the next clinic. She was eight months pregnant.

The fruit pickers in town stand out, even if not by racial characteristics. It's obvious that they don't belong. Maybe they are homeless: hobos in a park by the employment office, waiting for work. Maybe they are driving their trucks and trailers down the road with aluminum ladders on the top and out-of-state license plates. Because they are migrant, they are easy prey for the local police.

Across from the employment office, Wenatchee, Washington, 1977.

"The cops is the ones that can really treat the pickers bad," commented Daniel. "The other evening I was in Wenatchee at that park in town, and there were some guys sittin' around, and one old hobo was layin' on the ground. Then a cop car drives up and this cop starts pokin' on this guy with a stick to get him up. Well, he didn't budge, so that cop hit him really hard 'til he got up, and he moved him out into the street. Then they told everyone to move on, and those guys got their bedrolls and went down to the tracks. Anyone else but those winos woulda had a case against that cop."

"Just because those guys tramp around don't mean they don't deserve the same respect as anybody else," said Thelma.

"I guess I couldn't count how many times I've been stopped for out-of-state plates," said Travis. "That's the way they spot the pickers who ain't layin' around the park."

We could attest to that. We'd been stopped many, many times for our out-of-state plates. One time, after the apple harvest was over, we were warned that we had a week to get out of town. Another time Rick was stopped in Washington State because of his Oregon plates. His license had expired and he didn't know it. The police officer frisked him and then took him into jail. After he'd bailed himself out, he went to apply for a new license and was told he'd have to wait a week. Since we were leaving for the cherry harvest in Montana in a couple of days, he agreed to take the test for the permit. He was asked his address, and answered: "P.O. Box 261." "What city?" asked the examiner. "Wenatchee," answered Rick. "If you can't think of the answers quicker than that, you better go back to the end of the line," was the response. Rick asked for his money back, drove to Montana, and got a license there.

Daniel told another story of being stopped by a cop for having out-of-state plates. "He kept standing there making cracks and trying to get me to smart off to him, but I wouldn't say a word. Finally he said, 'Well, it really looks like snow today. I reckon it's going to snow.' And that day was just as clear as could

Left: *Pickers protest lack of adequate housing. Wenatchee, Washington, 1977.*

be, there wasn't a cloud in the sky, so I said, 'No, it doesn't look like snow today.'

"And just as soon as I said that, he said, 'Oh, tryin' to get smart with me, are ya? Well, I'll just show you—I'm taking you to the jail.' And he did, he took me to the jailhouse and it cost me ten

John Thomas, East Wenatchee, Washington, 1979.

dollars to bail myself out. And those were really hard times, we were living on those commodity beans. Every day, I'd take a pint jar of beans to work for my lunch. I'd go off and hide and eat my lunch for the other pickers wouldn't see me eatin' beans out of a fruit jar. Things were really hard and that guy took ten dollars away, just for nothing. That was a lot of money back then!"

Migrants are frequently associated with crime in the community. Although a large influx of people into an area at harvest time does make the possibility of crime greater, Okie migrants are responsible for very little of this criminal activity and deeply resent the association.

"I guess the picker who moves around a lot makes an easy scapegoat," commented Darlene. "Anytime any kind of crime goes on in the town, they blame it on the migrants. Did you see that story in the paper the other day about that old lady who was robbed and beaten up? They said she lives on the road the migrants use to go pick cherries on the Heights. Well, any cherry picker knows the cherries up there are a long ways from bein' ripe."

"It was the same way when that gal got killed up in Chelan," Ruby said. "Before they knowed anything about it, they was blamin' it on a 'transient' and talkin' about all the fruit pickers in town."

The town newspaper is the source of information for the community, and inaccurate or stereotypical information that is reported in the paper is a sore point with pickers. "Once a reporter came out to our camp to talk to us and we was all living in our trailers and campers, but it come out in the paper the next day that we was sleepin' under a bridge!" said Daniel.

It was dark in the camp by now and most of the trailer lights had been turned off. Only a few people remained talking outside.

Walter's brow was furrowed with concentration. "Maybe fruit pickers ain't the best group of people around, but I don't think they've ever been showed the right way to be treated," he said. "The farmer he works for is taking him for a ride, the people in the grocery stores will cheat him, and if a newspaper reporter comes out to do a story on him, that reporting won't be honest."

"That's right," agreed Travis. "Far as that goes, the fruit tramps make as honest a living as anybody and work harder than most people doin' it."

"We just move around, is all," Darlene said excitedly. "That don't make us criminals. I'd like to know how in the world they'd ever get their crops harvested if we didn't travel around the country doin' it for them!"

The group fell silent for a moment as if we had said it all. Then the sound of Hank's truck as it pulled slowly into the camp disrupted the stillness. Hank switched off his lights and eased the truck up beside his trailer. The inky blackness of the night seemed to surround us suddenly.

"Goodnight, ya'all," Hank called softly, as he stepped inside his door.

Far Left: *View from Stemilt Hill, Wenatchee, Washington, 1978.*

Left: *Rodney, Okanogan, Washington, 1979.*

15. "It Leaves an Ambitious Person in Kind of a Bad Way"
Migrants and the Government

After the last tree was picked on our cherry job in East Wenatchee, the pickers gathered around the foreman's mobile home at the edge of the orchard to wait for their checks. The grower filled washtubs with ice, soda pop, and beer for the pickers to enjoy as they waited.

Not long ago, the farmers used to throw real parties for the pickers at the end of harvest, complete with food, drinks, and general celebration. But such a festive event had become a rarity, and we felt grateful just for the cold drinks to mark our contribution to the crop's harvest.

The grower went inside the mobile home to write checks,

Left: *East Wenatchee, Washington, 1977.*

and one at a time, the pickers went inside to settle their accounts. The process took a long time because almost all the pickers wanted to be paid with checks no larger than a hundred and fifty dollars, to avoid paying social security tax. (At that time, checks under a hundred and fifty dollars were exempt from social security insurance.) For some large families who had done well on the job, this meant they would receive more than a dozen checks.

Although the pickers could have benefited from social security insurance in their old age, since there are no other retirement benefits in farmwork, they were too suspicious and cynical about the system to voluntarily pay into it. They wanted to have all the money they had earned right away. "Heck, I ain't gonna live that long anyways," said one picker as he explained why he didn't want money taken out of his check. Another picker expressed more doubt in the system itself: "By the time I reach sixty-five, there prob'ly won't be no social security nohow!"

Usually it was the women who went in to "settle up" with the grower. The other pickers washed their hands and faces with icy water from a spigot outside the mobile home, took cold cans of pop and beer from the ice bucket, and relaxed under the shade of the orchard trees to wait their turns.

The Thomases, four brothers and their families who had worked this job for years, formed the heart of this picking crew. They were known for their high picking standards and their witty rapport at work. Earl, with his squat body and round face covered with friendly wrinkles, was a contrast to his older brother Jack, who was taller and leaner with a rough leathery face.

As they settled under the trees with the other pickers, sitting on their cherry buckets or cross-legged on the ground, Earl turned to Jack. "Well, I sure hope you brought your chains to

Right: *Quincy, Washington, 1977.*

tow me out of this orchard—I didn't make enough on this job to buy my gas home."

Jack squinted and a wry smile formed on his lips. He took a puff on his cigarette before he spoke. "I can get you out, Earl," he drawled. "but I just want to make sure you don't come back next year. You look like one of them kinds of guys that keeps coming back for more."

There was laughter around the group that disguised their real financial worries. Jobs that used to be big money-makers had produced poor crops for years in a row, and all the lesser jobs in between vanished as these migrants were replaced by others. Usually the pickers are nonchalant about such matters. "We just hit a poverty pocket," they say, knowing that they'll pull through somehow. Yet they're aware that for all their hard work, they are only slightly better off than their counterparts receiving welfare.

Their self-respect as they struggle with poverty seems undermined by the availability of welfare, and fruit pickers often express resentment and hostility towards both the welfare system and its recipients. "Those welfare types" is a commonly accepted synonym for people who are too lazy to work. In addition, migrants like to joke about getting welfare themselves. These jokes are told in the company of other pickers, with the assumption that everyone knows they are kidding. In reality, they would consider welfare only in a severe economic crisis; their pride and their strong work ethic prevent them from taking advantage of the system.

"Myself, I wish Warren would be a social worker when he gets out of school," commented Cathy, a mother of three. "Then I'd be all fixed up—he could get me welfare and food stamps."

"I'd like to get into that welfare too," Earl said. "On the receiving end!"

Gladys set down her can of Diet Coke and grinned. "Well now, I believe in helpin' poor people. Lord, I wish somebody rich would help me!"

"Y'know, these farmers are the ones getting money from the government," said Cathy in a serious tone. "When they give it to the farmers they call it subsidies, but when they give it to the pickers they call it welfare." She paused a moment, then added, "Only they won't even give it to the pickers!"

The screen door of the mobile home shut as May walked out with several checks in her hand. Earl's wife, next in line, got up and walked to the mobile home as the pickers sitting under the trees teased May. "Well, I hope you didn't clean them out!" "Don't spend all that money in one place!"

May got into a pickup with her husband, Kenny, another of the Thomas brothers.

"Well, you got your white-line money!" Jack called.

"They're rich now—watch out!" kidded Earl, as Kenny and May drove off.

Our more serious conversations with migrant fruit pickers revealed some of the reasons for their deep distrust of government programs, including welfare. When we brought up the topic with Walter and Daniel one day, it was apparent that they'd thought about the subject at length.

"Life has become a little easier for migrant workers," Walter said as he reviewed the last thirty years he'd spent as a fruit picker. "But it's been through the efforts of the government. For instance, food stamps can help a person an awful lot, and it's easier to obtain credit now so you can buy things on credit that you couldn't buy back then. You may see people driving new cars and better trailers, but they still owe for those things. And with welfare and food stamps and unemployment insurance, people

are a little more secure in the knowledge that they can make those payments. But it didn't come from the farmer that they work for, and I think this is really a wrong thing. I think the welfare system has had a deteriorating effect on the migrant worker—it's taken his independence away. The security we have comes from the federal government, not from our jobs."

"Yeah, it leaves an ambitious person in kind of a bad way," agreed Daniel. "He can go out and work twice as much as somebody that's on welfare, and he will get exactly the same in the end." He stopped, searching for the appropriate analogy. "You take a mother—she might tell her daughter, 'You go in there and do the dishes, and I'll give you a dollar, or if you don't do the dishes, well, I'll give you a dollar anyway.' Well, it's gonna be a rare little girl who goes in there and does them dishes. That's kinder the way it is with fruit pickers and welfare."

Left and Above: *Cherry orchard meeting, Stockton, California, 1977.*

"It seems like a lot of farmers have the impression that migrant workers are nothing but a lazy bunch drawing welfare," said Walter. "But if they could only stop and consider a minute, that there's actually more money in welfare than there is in their fruit orchards, maybe the wages could come up a little bit to entice people to work better. People don't like to work for nothing! They just don't have any compunction whatsoever to go out there and break their backs when there's an easier way to do it."

I asked Walter what he'd do to solve the problem, and his answer was typically impassioned.

"For myself, I'd like to see a complete end put to the welfare system. But that has got to come about through paying people for their work. Until there is a better way, then the welfare system is the only thing we've got to go on, I guess, but I'd like for people to be able to make their own way, so that they can stand proud and tall. I don't think there's anyone who has a better reason to be proud than those people who supply food to this nation, both the farmer and the people who work for him," Walter concluded.

The issue of pride is at the core of the Okie migrant culture, and it is why many migrants are resentful and suspicious of government programs and handouts. Although they use food stamps when they're out of work, it's only a temporary measure to help them get through periods of seasonal unemployment. They may use migrant or community clinics (which serve the community's low-income population as well) but only as an emergency measure. Here, too, they are sensitive to any disrespect for migrants that they may receive along with the reduced-fee services. Instead of being grateful for such services, they're apt to feel resentful that their economic position forces them to endure long waits in crowded waiting rooms and cursory visits with various doctors, rather than consistent, considerate medical care.

Fruit pickers commonly express their resentment at the bandage solutions of government through cynical jokes or limited use of such programs. Government programs often seem to reinforce the idea that farm work is work that no one would choose, and that there isn't enough money in agriculture to pay workers appropriate wages and benefits. The very existence of such programs implies that solutions can't be found within the work system itself.

Mistrust of government frequently leads migrants to behave in a devious manner towards officials. One day we were in a migrant camp when people from the Migrant Education program came to inform pickers about a free health-insurance program for children. They approached some teenagers who were hanging around outside the trailers and asked if they could speak with their parents. "I don't know," one of the boys said, with mock seriousness. "Some other people just went in and he kicked them out. If I were you, I wouldn't go in—my dad's arms are as big as your legs!"

The kids, who ranged in age from thirteen to sixteen, also told the visitors that they were all married and had children of their own—another fib, since none of them did. Discouraged, the Migrant Education people turned away, without going to the other trailers. The kids went to tell their parents about the successful trick they'd played, and their parents joined them in a hearty laugh.

Later, when we learned that the Migrant Education people had been taking a survey of how many people were at the camp, I could only speculate as to how innacurate it must have been. They never verified the teenagers' claims, never knew how many people were in the trailers or were in town at the time they came by. Like many other statistics on migrants, the survey could not have had much basis in fact.

Other experiences in dealing with government programs

March for migrant housing, Wenatchee, Washington, 1977.

gave us a taste of the frustration and hopelessness that fruit pickers feel with such attempts to help them. Once, we applied for help with school tuition through Northwest Rural Opportunities, an organization established to help migrants leave farm work by means of education or training. First we had to fill out reams of paperwork, which seemed inappropriate in itself since many migrants are functionally illiterate or have only an elementary education. Then, after several appointments, we were told that the organization was low on funds and had only enough to maintain its office and staff. But what purpose was served by having the office and staff remain? we wondered. On paper, it looked as if the organization was helping migrants but in reality it helped only its own employees.

Even programs that are largely beneficial, such as Migrant Education, spend a large percentage of their funds on conventions, lunches, and hotels. Migrants are acutely aware that the kind of life led by employees of these organization is a far cry from their own, and they feel that the government funds support such middle-class lifestyles more than they alleviate poverty among migrant workers.

In addition, many migrant programs are oriented toward helping Spanish-speaking migrants. This is necessary and appropriate but tends to further alienate Okie migrants. The organizations that are supposed to help them are often geared toward Hispanics. Here too, as in the job market, Anglo migrants feel neglected and ignored—almost invisible.

Mount Hood, Oregon, 1978.

The migrants' distrust of government extends to the fear that government interference may actually make things worse for them. In fact, this has often been the case. Occupational Safety and Health Act (OSHA) laws that sought to improve housing conditions for pickers only resulted in migrant housing being torn down by growers to avoid compliance. Child labor laws designed to protect migrant children had the effect of breaking up the family unit and preventing many families from continuing on the fruit run. Laws requiring social security benefits for migrants have resulted in smaller paychecks for migrants who may never experience social security benefits. In short, migrants rarely experience a law or government program that truly does benefit them without stripping them of their pride.

"Migrants have always resented an interference by the government," Walter said. "Migrants want to be able to come and go and to live their own lives without interference from anyone—even someone who's tryin' to help them."

The bottom line is that most Okie migrants want to be able to help themselves, through their own honest labor. "To me, a person is alive only if he'll do something to help himself and his people," Walter told us. "If he just lives to get food on the table that night and doesn't ever do anything to improve himself, he's just a vegetable. We all want to do something to help ourselves, even if some of us don't care about driving fancy new cars or living in new houses."

Once You Know It's There,
You Never Forget It
Down the Road

16. "I Already Had to Give Up California, and I May Have to Give Up the Rest Pretty Soon Too"
Settling Out and Moving On

Left: *Winterhaven, Florida, 1974.*

In the late summer, when there was a lull in the available fruit work, we stayed in a campground in Walla Walla, Washington, and drove the dusty orchard roads looking for work. At last we found a few days of work in nearby Milton-Freewater, Oregon. The August days were as ripe and heavy as the blue-violet Italian prunes we gathered into our picking sacks. We suffered the sweltering heat, swarms of gnats milling around our faces, tall grass that made moving our ladders difficult, and stickers that jabbed at our skin through the thick trousers we wore—all for a job that paid very little and lasted for fewer days than it had taken to find it.

Whatever reasons people usually gave for choosing the life of a fruit picker seemed to fade during this rough time of late summer. Many days of waiting and looking for work were interspersed with a few miserable jobs in the prunes or the pears that helped us scrape by. People began to talk about leaving the fruit run for good as they confronted all the worst aspects of their chosen work.

Bob Malloy, who lived in a tiny, fifteen-foot trailer with his wife and three teenaged children, had reached the point of disgust. "I already had to give up California, and I may have to give up the rest pretty soon too," he said. "Everything is getting too high—everything but wages. What I hate is all these days with no work, when you got a big family to feed. They all got to eat every day, whether you work or not. Rain or shine, you gotta eat."

Bob's sentiments were echoed by many fruit pickers in the campground. People complained bitterly, as they seldom did when there was good work around. Some of them would change their minds the next spring and be back on the road. But every year more and more of them really did leave, and unlike in years past, now it was difficult to get back once you left. Fewer jobs remained open every year, and for those that remained there was intense competition. "You can't hardly buy a job," Bob complained. "The Mexicans has got all the jobs and a white person can't get in."

The jobs that are left picking fruit often pay poorly and require a picker to work in ways that he or she would have refused to do in the past, such as color-picking (picking only part

Right: *Pears, Cashmere, Washington, 1974.*

of the tree at a time) or accepting unfair methods of allocating trees or sections of the orchard to pickers. "Anymore a fruit picker can't be as choosy as he useta could," commented Billie.

Okie pickers have been most affected by the influx of undocumented Hispanic workers to the fruit orchards of California and the Northwest. Even penalties for employers who knowingly hire undocumented workers have failed to change the situation. After an initial panic at the new regulations, growers became used to giving their workers long forms to fill out at the beginning of each job. As long as these forms were completed, the employer was in the clear—and no one was the wiser if falsified information was given on the forms. In an apple orchard where I worked last fall, virtually all of the pickers were working illegally, despite the supposedly rigorous regulations.

Not only the Okies have been adversely affected by the widespread use of *illegales* in agriculture. Chicano friends of ours expressed strong conflicts about Mexicans who entered the United States illegally to find work. They helped relatives come up north and locate work, even though they felt as if they were cutting their own throats to do so. Aristello Diaz, who does year-round field work in Madras, Oregon, and used to pick fruit in the summer as well, told us, "We didn't work in the garlic this year, because there was a contractor come up from California. He brought up a crew of wetbacks and all the people who lived here and worked here before couldn't get a job. It's the same way in the fruit. We used to go over to Hood River and stay there three, four months. We'd pick cherries and we'd thin apples, we'd pick pears and apples. Now you can't get a job there anymore; it's all wetbacks. I wish they wouldn't let them come up here anymore."

Aristello talked to us in his dilapidated old trailer home, where the smell of freshly cooked tortillas wafted through the tiny rooms. His grandchildren were giggling, yelling and talking in a mixture of Spanish and English. Aristello's wife, Adelina, admonished the children from time to time: "*Deja lo!* Leave that alone!" as she rolled tortillas from the soft flour dough. She put down her rolling pin for a moment to join the conversation.

"And in Madras, why should we try to save our money to buy a house," she asked, "when we can't even get a job here anymore? The wetback, he can come up here and work a few months, then he can live for a year in Mexico. But living up here, you only make enough for tomorrow, and then you don't have nothing."

Aristello and Adelina are among those who have quit following the migrant fruit harvest, even though they are still involved with farm work. They live with the economic contradictions inherent in their situation: the strains of helping support family members who come north to find work coupled with the hardships of finding work themselves because of these competitive workers.

The use of workers from Mexico is not recent; it is the escalation of a process that began in the 1940s. In 1941, when many Okies left agricultural labor to work in the burgeoning defense industry of the cities, they were soon replaced by Mexican workers under the bracero program. Though this program failed, Mexican workers continued to come, most illegally. In recent years, they have been joined by many from Central America.

The children of the Okies who stayed in farm work in the 1940s are particularly nostalgic about the old days when work was plentiful and growers were grateful to find available laborers. Daniel Williams traveled with his family in the 1940s, leaving and later coming back to fruit picking as an adult. Sitting on his cherry bucket during a coffee break in the orchard, Daniel absently kicked a clod of dirt and reminisced: "I like the fruit run so much that I wish it was like it used to be. Not altogether like it used to be, but like the different places that we used to go. Like those pea patches that'd go right out to the ocean in California. I know a lot of the reason we can't go back is because it's all built up around there, but also it's because all the people there think Americans don't want to do that work, and they won't make it be good enough so somebody does want to do it."

Virgil England, who heads a large clan of fruit-picking families, recollected, "When we started working thirty-three years ago, you could go anywhere and get a job. Pick cotton in the winter, stripping the bolls until March. Then we'd be thinning peaches or plums and then it'd be time for the cherries again. Now it's getting hard to find a job. One job we had in The Dalles [Oregon] we'd worked for thirteen years, and one year the farmer just hired all Mexicans, and we couldn't work there no more."

Some migrants who decide to leave the run and "settle out" already have other skills that they can turn into jobs. Mostly these are blue-collar jobs like mechanic, carpenter, or welder. Often women will remain in farm work, choosing nonmigratory but still seasonal work in the packing sheds or canneries. Some, like Joyce, try to get training in another line of work so they can leave the fruit run. During the winter in Exeter, California, she enrolled in a cooks' training course, part of a training program designed for migrants. The course turned out to be basic instructions on being a fry-cook. Joyce got bored and quit after three months of the five-month course. She took a job at a drive-in but quit after two weeks because her boss was overly particular about appearance.

Many times fruit pickers find themselves unable to adapt to the kinds of jobs available outside of agriculture. The formal process of applying for a job—filling out forms, having résumés with references, education, and experience—is foreign to them, after the casualness of farm work. Likewise, the ongoing stability and stifling of self-expression required by jobs that are often unpleasant or by bosses who can be disagreeable runs against the grain of migrants who have always relied on leaving when things look bad. The low wages paid in most work that poorly educated migrants qualify for provide no compensation for the lack of mobility and freedom that come with stable hourly work.

"I think once you pick fruit for a few years, you get used to workin' for a few days and then bein' off for a few days," one picker told us. "It gets in your blood and you can't work a steady job."

Often, instead of leaving the fruit run, a migrant will try to better him or herself by becoming a contractor, running a crew of pickers. When our friend Bill saw his pride as a fruit picker turn to bitterness, as he witnessed the deterioration of the working conditions and his own health, he decided to try to become a contractor. His best friend had made this transition from cherry picker to contractor successfully, and there were many of the old pickers who continued to pick fruit on some of the jobs and run others as contractors.

But Bill soon grew frustrated with the pressures of trying to contract orchard work. It's a job where one has to manage people, to the satisfaction of no one. He began to seek other alternatives to traditional work. For a couple of years he dreamed and talked of going to Alaska with his family—he wanted to experience what he called the New Frontier. Meanwhile, he kept picking fruit but his work was getting more haphazard. He criticized and antagonized co-workers and bosses and worked sporadically, coming to work late and taking hour-long coffee breaks.

His behavior was intentional. After he had earned a bad reputation on a job he'd worked for many years, he said, "I fixed it so I can never go back." He told us that it was his last season, and that it had been harder to leave fruit picking than he thought. He'd decided to ruin it for himself so that he would never want to

go back. "You can't leave something when it's that good," he said. "You've got to ruin it first."

After our last cherry job for that year ended, Bill and his wife, Vicki, gave us their two cherry buckets as a symbolic gesture—they were quitting the cherry run for good, they thought. The next year Bill went to Alaska with his son and then returned; then he and Vicki bought a fishing boat with money from the sale of their trailer. They lived on the Washington coast and tried to make a go at fishing. But they faced new problems in fishing, and they worked in fish canneries to make ends meet. After several years, they sold their boat. They worked as window washers and sign painters in the winter and then returned to orchard country to pick fruit in the summers. Bill had not permanently damaged his reputation after all—through old friends on the fruit run he could still find some work.

The ties that bind fruit pickers to their work are strong, and for each tie that is negative, there is one that is positive—one the flip side of the other. Economic dependence is coupled with job independence; instability is wed to freedom; uprootedness is offset by deep connectedness to family and friends.

Bill's return to fruit picking was similarly mixed. After his absence, he defined himself less as a fruit picker than as a person who could make money at a variety of jobs. Since he felt less economically dependent and more removed from the migrant life, he could approach the work with less bitterness and disappointment. He was able to change his old style of picking fruit at a breakneck pace, to adjust the work for his age and physical capacities.

Perhaps in many ways Bill could appreciate fruit picking that much more because he'd let go of so many of his expectations. But he still noticed that things had continued to change for

Left: *Heading off to work, Benton City, Washington, 1977.*

"You only make enough for tomorrow, and then you don't have nothing." Aristello Diaz, Cashmere, Washington, 1975.

stopped showing pickers the courtesy they once had. "They don't never carry your ladders no more," one picker noted.

The old crews Bill had worked with were largely gone, and so was the old spirit. "The crew here used to have a real spirit," Bill said of a job we'd worked together in years past. "That's why you'd work here. That would just give you the spirit to go up that hill! Now all the old pickers are gone, and it's just us. Even Frank said it's his last time. 'They can have it!' he said." The reason Bill couldn't define himself as a fruit picker anymore doesn't lie in the work itself; it has to do with that spirit. The sense of pride that fruit pickers value so highly has suffered under such repeated blows to the spirit.

Still, Bill and Vicki have been able to return to fruit picking with renewed enthusiasm themselves because of their ability to adapt to the changes that have occurred. "Each year I love it more and more," Vicki said of picking. "Especially the cherry picking. But now you never know what you'll find when you come back. A lot of the old jobs have really changed for the worse."

Bill and Vicki have been able to adapt to the fact that they now work in predominantly Hispanic crews, and their past resentment of this fact is quite distinct from the genuine respect and admiration they hold for their co-workers. "Now I'm talking to them," Bill said. "I like these people. At first they wouldn't hardly look at me—they'd keep a certain face—not too friendly or too unfriendly. They're shy really, almost afraid of you. And I used to have this bad feeling too about them bein' here, but it was never towards the people. I knew if I was them I'd be doin' the same thing."

When a Mexican foreman took over one of the old cherry jobs, he changed the methods of distributing the work. Once this

the worse while he'd been away. It was harder to get a job, and he'd worked one job in California where they had to pick the same trees three times—"color picking"—something he would have quit over years ago. He noticed other changes on the old jobs—things were less fair, the contractors and tractor driver's

Right: *Making tortillas, Madras, Oregon, 1979.*

last season, when there weren't enough rows of apples for all the pickers on the crew, he told Bill, "'I'll just flip a coin—tails, the whites get it; heads the Mexicans get it,'" Bill related. "At first I let it go by, thinking at least he had the element of luck in it. Because I'd been trying to tell him about drawing for rows, that you gotta have the element of luck. I'd tell him, 'Let me curse my luck, not curse you!' But Vicki said, 'Bill, he can't flip between the Mexicans and the whites. That's not right.' And when I thought about it, I thought, 'No, you'll lose all that ground we've gained the last few years—you'll start a war out there.' Fortunately, Gerald came out and told him, 'You can't do that. We're not two crews— we're one crew. You have to do it fair.'"

Ability to adapt and get along with the new crew is some insurance for Bill and Vicki that they will be welcome at least on the jobs that they've worked the last few seasons. Finding new work is more difficult and often a challenge.

Even those people who decide to leave the fruit run permanently cherish the idea that the work will still be there when they need it. Walter quit the fruit run years ago, and his brother followed a couple of years later, when they found steady year-round work in Texas, and it no longer seemed feasible to support their large families by fruit picking. They both have a deep nostalgia for the fruit run and express a desire to return to it someday if they can.

Several years ago Walter told us, "There's a lot of people who leave the run for awhile and then come back to it. Seems like if you know it's there you never forget it. I left it for ten years, but even when I was working in the plywood mill, I'd go out and pick grapes on my days off. If I was out of work, I'd go south and grab a ladder and work with my folks. And a lot of people will marry out of the fruit run altogether, marry someone who's never done it at all. But if they have a crisis or lose everything they have, then a lot of times they'll go back to the fruit."

"You can't leave something when it's that good. You've got to ruin it first." Bill and Vicki Taylor, Finley Point, Montana, 1976.

Right: *Red Delicious apples, Cashmere, Washington, 1972.*

The idea of being able to return to the fruit run at any time has less reality with each passing year. Each year has eroded a part of the fruit run that Okies used to travel. Another town—Hood River or Salem, Oregon; Natchez or Wenatchee Heights, Washington—is scratched off the map as a place to find work. Important contacts disappear as more Okie contractors and co-workers leave, and growers become accustomed to more homogeneous crews of Hispanic pickers.

The fruit picker who does try to stay faces intense competition for jobs, increased expenses, wages that don't keep up with inflation and often actually go down, and the continued bias of the larger culture toward pickers. Among those who stay there is always talk of leaving, and the joking manner scarcely conceals their real discontent.

"Reckon I oughta be able to buy a bucket cheap today!" Slim called through the orchard during a particularly hard day in a scrappy section of the cherry orchard.

"Naw, I'll keep my old cherry bucket," Charlie responded. "Whenever I get finished with all this cherry picking, I'm gonna get it chromed and plant flowers in it."

Motivated mainly by nostalgia and a real love for the migrant life and work, some Okies continue to pick fruit even after they are no longer economically dependent on the income from it—attesting to the element of choice in their decision to pick fruit. Others cling to the fruit run because of the limitations of their choices: illiteracy, lack of education or job training, alcoholism, or other problems can prevent them from seeking other kinds of work and force them to stay with what they have even as it worsens.

Out of the dozen or so families that we knew at our regular job in the cherries, only a couple of families returned this last year. Some of the older pickers had health reasons for not returning, and some of the younger ones had found other kinds of work that they couldn't leave. "You wouldn't want to give up a steady job for this," Earl told us. But years ago, that is exactly what we *did* want to do, and we thought the benefits then outweighed the disadvantages.

As we have moved into other kinds of work—Rick as a newspaper reporter, I as a craftsperson and writer—I find that it becomes harder each harvest season to keep my own ties to fruit picking alive. Returning to an old job can be a lonely and discour-

"They don't never carry your ladders no more." Pasco, Washington, 1976.

aging experience, when the pickers you used to know are gone. Placed by myself in an isolated section of orchard on a cherry job this last summer, I listened to distant calls in Spanish and realized the feeling of alienation that the last Okie fruit pickers must also experience.

The history of the Okies and the history of farm work continue in their own ways, but now they take divergent paths. That particular marriage of the Okie subculture and migratory farm work that began in the 1930s will soon be just a memory. To mainstream society, its dissolution is a small, almost imperceptible loss. But to those who knew it, the loss is greater; it wrenches the heart. For it was an intimate marriage, rich with human experience. It won't be soon forgotten.

17. My Fingers Miss the Feelin' of Those Cherry-Pickin' Times
Postscript

It's taken over eighteen years to bring this work to fruition, and as I write this postscript I am struck by how much has changed and how many losses we have sustained. I'm also moved and renewed as I read again the words of the pickers themselves—those words have lost none of their power and expressiveness. Where my own writing has sometimes failed me, the voices of the fruit pickers we worked with never have. They have always told of their lives with dignity and raw honesty.

The way of life we knew as migrant fruit pickers has not completely disappeared, but the sense of choice, of freedom and pride, has been sadly diminished. The constant oversupply of

Left: *Making pies, Seattle, Washington, 1974.*

workers for years on end has cut the availability of jobs to the point where it is no longer economically feasible to travel so far with a family and a trailer across the country for work in the fields. Worse than that is the pervasive sense of shame and degradation that migrants have had to suffer in the eyes of the society at large. What continues to amaze me is that they've held on to their pride, their self-worth, their integrity, and their own sense of the value of their work.

I'm also struck by the fact that the only "solution" that has ever been proposed to make life better for migrants is to help them get out of the migrant stream. Why does our society as a whole assume that work in the fields is without value? Working as a fruit picker for nearly two decades, I reconnected with my peasant roots and found a way of life that was rich in aesthetics and experience, both with nature and with people. I know all that is wrong and rotten about the way migrants are treated in this country, but I still can't believe that anything is wrong or rotten with harvesting the nation's fruits and vegetables.

Yet as the Okies leave agricultural work, I don't know if there will be another group of people to replace them as committed to or as proud of the migrant life and work. Perhaps society will always view the harvest as a "harvest of shame," without really exploring how our most basic assumptions perpetuate the shame associated with it. My hope is that this book can, through the perceptions and reflections of Okie migrants, challenge such assumptions and make us look at migrant agricultural workers with a fresh eye.

Rick and Toby, Okanogan, Washington, 1978.

My Fingers Miss the Feelin' of Those Cherry-Pickin' Times

Okies and Arkies and all kinds of fruit tramps,
They all get together each June,
To pick the ripe cherries from Lodi to Polson,
And go on to pick in the prunes.

But my fingers miss the feelin' of those cherry-pickin' times,
When my bucket was a-fillin' and my hands were a-flyin'.
Now the cherry pickin's over, and the fruit tramps are gone,
And it's time that this old tramp was movin' on.

I worked with my fam'ly in the beans and the cotton,
Till we were replaced by machines.
And mama said, "Daddy, I know somethin's rotten,
When you can't find a job in the beans."

From row crops to tree tops, we followed the seasons—
Our home was a highway lane.
But stayin' together was enough of a reason,
To go out on the road once again.

And my fingers miss the feelin' of those cherry-pickin' times,
When my bucket was a-fillin' and my hands were a-flyin'.
Now the cherry pickin's over and the fruit tramps are gone,
And it's time this old tramp was movin' on.

Well, we kept on pickin' till Daddy died one day;
We buried him under the trees.
Then I quit the fruit run and started a new run,
Chasing American dreams.

With a home in the suburbs, a TV, an RV,
I thought I had made it at last.
But no amount of buyin' will make up for the dyin',
Of a good way of life that has passed.

And my fingers miss the feelin' of those cherry-pickin' times,
When my bucket was a-fillin' and my hands were a-flyin'.
Now the cherry pickin's over and the fruit tramps are gone,
And it's time that this old tramp was movin' on.

—— *song written by Toby Sonneman.*

Apricots, Crescent Bar, Washington, 1975.

Notes

Chapter 2: "It Just Gets in Your Blood"—History of Okie Migrants

1. Paul Taylor, "Origins of Migratory Labor in the Wheat Belts of the Middle West and California: Second Half of the Nineteenth Century," in U.S. Senate Subcommittee on Migratory Labor, *Migrant and Seasonal Farmworker Powerlessness* (1971), part 8-C, 6761–62. See also Stephen H. Sosnick, *Hired Hands: Seasonal Farm Workers in the United States* (Santa Barbara, Calif.: McNally & Loftin, 1978).

2. John Steinbeck, *The Grapes of Wrath* (New York: Viking, 1939), 316.

3. Louisa R. Shotwell, *The Harvesters: The Story of the Migrant People* (New York: Doubleday, 1961), 74.

4. *Their Blood Is Strong*, by John Steinbeck (San Francisco: The Simon J. Lubin Society of California, 1938), was reprinted in its entirety in *A Companion to "The Grapes of Wrath,"* assembled and edited by Warren French (New York: Viking, 1963), 90.

5. Steinbeck, *The Grapes of Wrath*, 317–18.

6. Ibid., 280.

7. Gerald Haslam, "What about the Okies?" in *American History Illustrated*, April 1977, 29.

8. John Blanchard, *Caravans to the Northwest* (Boston: Houghton Mifflin, 1940), 30.

9. Ibid.

10. Ibid., 32.

11. Ibid., 37.

12. Steinbeck, *The Grapes of Wrath*, 346.

13. Blanchard, *Caravans to the Northwest*, 45.

14. Ibid., 44.

15. Steinbeck, *Their Blood is Strong*, quoted in French, *Companion*, 71.

16. Blanchard, *Caravans to the Northwest*, 46.

17. Roy Emerson Stryker and Nancy Wood, *In This Proud Land: America, 1935–1943, As Seen in the FSA Photographs* (New York: New York Graphic Society, 1973), 14.

18. Blanchard, *Caravans to the Northwest*, 43.

19. Sosnick, *Hired Hands*, 389.

20. Steve Allen, *The Ground Is Our Table* (New York: Doubleday, 1966), 63.

21. Ibid., 64.

22. Ibid.

23. Ibid., 67.

Chapter 3: "Seems Like I'd Like to Hear Those Old Buick Tires Hum Again"—Following the Harvests

1. Quoted in Sosnick, *Hired Hands*, 156.

2. Jack McQuarrie, *Wildcrafting: Harvesting the Wilds for a Living* (Santa Barbara, Calif.: Capra Press, 1975), 35–36.

3. Okla Slim, *The Hobo*, Winter 1990. The article in this periodical, published in Beverly, Washington, begins with an obituary (or poem):

    Hood River Blakie

    Bones

    Chicken Red

and reads underneath: "Caught the westbound." "Blakie" is perhaps misspelled; "Blackie" would be a more common hobo name.

Chapter 6: "Ain't Nobody Owns Me"—Pickers and Growers

1. Geraldine Warner, "Pruning, training, location are big factors in cherry culture," *Good Fruit Grower*, 15 May 1990, 22–23.

2. Camille Hukari, "Orchard worker satisfaction and personnel management," *Good Fruit Grower*, 1 May 1990, 29–32.

3. Ibid., 32.

Chapter 8: "You Meet All Kinds of People"—The Migrant Camp

1. McQuarrie, *Wildcrafting*, 39.

2. Ibid.

Chapter 14: "We're a Part of Feeding These People Who Have This Contempt for Us"—Migrants and the Community

1. Steinbeck, *Their Blood is Strong*, quoted in French, *Companion*, 54–55.

Selected Sources

Allen, Steve. *The Ground Is Our Table*. New York: Doubleday, 1966.

Blanchard, John. *Caravans to the Northwest*. Boston: Houghton Mifflin, 1940.

French, Warren, ed. *A Companion to "The Grapes of Wrath."* New York: Viking, 1963.

Ganzel, Bill. *Dust Bowl Descent*. Lincoln: University of Nebraska Press, 1984.

Haslam, Gerald. "What about the Okies?" in *American History Illustrated*, April 1977, 29.

McQuarrie, Jack. *Wildcrafting: Harvesting the Wilds for a Living*. Santa Barbara, Calif.: Capra Press, 1975.

Shotwell, Louisa R. *The Harvesters: The Story of the Migrant People*. New York: Doubleday, 1961.

Solkoff, Joel. *The Politics of Food*. San Francisco: Sierra Club Books, 1985.

Sosnick, Stephen H. *Hired Hands: Seasonal Farm Workers in the United States*. Santa Barbara, Calif.: McNally & Loftin, 1978.

Stein, Walter J. *California and the Dust Bowl Migration*. Westport, Conn.: Greenwood Press, 1973.

Steinbeck, John, *The Grapes of Wrath*. New York: Viking, 1939.

———. *Their Blood Is Strong*. San Francisco: The Simon J. Lubin Society of California, 1938. Reprinted in *A Companion to "The Grapes of Wrath."* Edited by Warren French. New York: Viking, 1963.

Stryker, Roy Emerson and Nancy Wood. *In This Proud Land: America, 1935–1943, As Seen in the FSA Photographs*. New York: New York Graphic Society, 1973.